VACATIONLAND TERRORISTS

Alarm in the Countryside

A Novel of Intrigue

FRANCIS DILLON

Published by BookLocker.com, Inc., Bradenton, Florida.

Printed in the United States of America on acid-free paper.

The characters and events in this book are fictitious. Any similarity to real persons, living or dead, is coincidental and not intended by the author.

BookLocker.com, Inc.
2014

First Edition

For our daughter-in-law Lauren, a superb editor, and my wife Judy, without whom this book would not be possible.

I also want to acknowledge a 91 years-young lady, Ollie, who urged me on to write this story.

Principal Characters Appearing in this Book

Grand City Mall
Security Officers Melanie, Gloria and Charles

Department of Homeland Security
Margaret Bollino, Director
William Wolsey, Deputy Director
Scott Hartley, Operations Chief
Richard Sandelman, Chief, Current Analysis Branch
Doug Foreman, Chief, Preliminary Inquiries Branch
Melissa Wallis, Night Supervisor, Operations Center
Ken Booth, team chief in Vermont
Albert Young, team member in Vermont
Bruce Thompson, team member in Vermont

The Berwick Group
Patrick Draper, partner in the firm
Nola Hunter, partner in the firm
John Carver, technical services director
Amanda Gillhooly, office manager
Ayman Siede, consultant used in Maine
Dr. Nancy McCray, source recruited in Vermont

U.S. Based-Terrorist Related Characters
Destiny Carter, law student and owner of farm in Maine
Binjamin "Ben" Panich, boyfriend of Destiny
Dr. Akil Hakimi, visiting professor from Egypt
Aarif Sawalha, aka; Josef Knowing, Imam from New Jersey
Sheikh Al Sakhr, Chief Imam of mosque in Newark, NJ
Ghanem, aka: Leroy Smith, explosives technician
Nasheed, female housekeeper for terrorists in Maine

Foreign Based -Terrorist Drivers
Umar and Awad Hussein, students from Yemen

Naseef Al Shuaibi, alleged student, entered from Canada
Nasir Ahmed, alleged student, entered from Canada
Samir Dahar, a baker, entered from St. Maarten
Rabiah Abdou, a cook, entered from St. Maarten

Maine Characters
John Hartwell, manager of Destiny's farm
Ginny Longley, nee: Paine, Destiny's friend, married to Tom Longley
Mrs. & Mrs. Paine, Ginny Longley's parents; owners of grocery store/garage at Paine's Corner

Maine Law Enforcement Personnel
Mark Daniels, Police Chief in Portland
Roger Tate, County Sheriff
Wally Barnes, Detective in Sheriff's office
Captain Dan Bowman, Maine State Police
Lieutenant Bill Goss, Maine State Police
Tom Longley, Maine State Police

New Hampshire Law Enforcement Personnel
Hal Manner, Sheriff
Horace Cobb, Deputy, Sheriff's department

PROLOGUE

The midnight shift change of security officers at the Grand City Mall in the southeast section of Cleveland, Ohio, went smoothly. The departing officers reported a quiet evening; closing had been routine, and a sweep of the entire facility had not detected anyone hiding in the public facilities. The warm spring weather had flushed the homeless vagrants out into the streets and parks of the city. Thus the mall regained the quiet but eerie posture when a security officer made a routine patrol through the darkened corridors, clocking in at the various check points in the building.

The overnight shift consisted of three security officers: one to monitor the vast array of cameras, both inside the mall and in the outer parking areas; one to walk the corridors on an hourly routine; and one to patrol the outer perimeter of the mall and the vast parking area. The mall was built in the shape of a cross, anchored by four large department stores at the end of each cross section. It was two stories high with over 150 specialty shops, restaurants, and vendor wagons. There was a large atrium where the four corridors of the mall intersected. This area was devoted for special events and holiday celebrations such as Santa-Land during the Christmas season.

This evening the youngest of the three security officers, Melanie, was given the cameras and communications position so she could study for an upcoming final exam at the community college she attended. That meant Gloria, a middle-aged divorcee, would take the patrol route inside the building. The women alternated these two positions because Charles, a retired police officer and shift supervisor, always patrolled the outside area in an enclosed golf cart. While the neighborhood surrounding the mall was normally quiet and safe at night, Charles felt more comfortable with his female colleagues working the inside positions. The history of the mall was that most all the security troubles occurred when the mall was open. Except for finding an occasional vagrant hiding in one of the public bathrooms, the overnight shift was pretty boring- that's why Melanie could study while she occasionally scanned the security cameras.

So far, it had been a very quiet evening, and, as time passed to the early morning hours, Charles parked his golf cart and proceeded into the central security office for a coffee break. It was 3:10 AM, and Melanie was still hard at work reviewing her class notes. As Charles stirred milk into his coffee, he glanced up at the cameras for the outside area, which were set on a rotating cycle to cover specific zones around the building. As one camera rotated views of the north parking area, he noticed a car parked up on the sidewalk against the large entrance doors of the building. He reached over and froze the picture.

"Melanie, didn't you notice that car drive up to the doors?"

"What car?" she said, as she looked up and became startled at the frozen camera picture of a car flush against the entrance doors. "I was looking at the cameras just before you came in and didn't see anything."

"Well, it didn't fly into the parking lot. Here, reverse that camera and let me see the sequence of that particular zone for the previous 10 minutes."

Melanie did as Charles ordered. The time-lapse review showed a car coming into the camera's position at 3:07 AM. The camera sensors were programmed to focus on movement, and thus followed the car as it was pulled up onto the sidewalk and parked against the entrance doors. The next sequence at 3:09 AM showed what appeared to be a male fleeing the car and running through the parking area out into the public street. He was dressed in jeans, wearing sneakers and a hooded sweatshirt, which blocked a good shot of his face. The camera at this point shifted back from following the male and began its rotating sweep of the north parking area.

Charles keyed his portable radio and said, "Gloria, where are you in the building?"

"I just left station 14 and have started into the north wing. Is there a problem?"

"Yes, but I'm not sure what it is. Someone parked a car up against the north entrance doors and just ran away."

"Why would anyone leave a car there?" said Gloria.

"Damned if I know." He turned and said, "Melanie, call the police dispatcher and tell them to send a patrol car to the north side of the mall. I'll meet them there."

"Should I call the mall manager too? Our procedures say we should call management if we have any unusual incidents."

"No, let's wait until the police get here and we figure out what is going on. Then we can make our calls. I am going around to meet Gloria." He keyed his radio again and told Gloria to walk up to the north entrance doors and unlock them and wait for him.

As Charles drove the golf cart around to the north side of the building, there was a blinding flash and explosion. Heat and debris rained around him and onto the metal roof of the golf cart. He instinctively ducked, and the hard plastic windshield of the cart protected his face. Fortunately, his old police habit of wearing a vest had helped, too. He didn't notice, but several pieces of debris hit him, slicing though his uniform and causing surface cuts on his legs and arms. He stared in amazement. In all his years on the police force he never had encountered such an explosion. What had been an automobile had disintegrated into a fiery shower of plastic and metal covering the parking lot and blowing away the doors and display windows of the building. He finally regained his composure and yelled into his radio. "Melanie, call 911! We need fire and police and an ambulance here now."

"I've already called them. I also tried to contact Gloria, but she doesn't answer." Should I go down there?"

"No. You stay at your post because you are the central point of communications. I am going back to a side entrance between the atrium and the north building and work my way down to the north wing to find Gloria. I'll call you when I get there. I'll leave the side door open and you direct the medics there."

"Okay, Charles. God, I'm scared, and it's my entire fault. I should have seen that car. I never dreamed we would have a car explode in the mall."

"Don't go crazy on me, Melanie. Just stay there and direct everyone when they arrive. No one could have done anything after the car was parked there. It probably had a timer on it. I'm starting down the hallway now to find Gloria. You just keep calm."

CHAPTER ONE

William Wolsey, the Deputy Director of the Department of Homeland Security and his Operations Chief, Scott Hartley, entered the classified conference room and took their appointed seats for the morning stand-up briefing. On his first day of duty six months ago, he wondered why the morning briefing was called stand-up, since they always sat for the briefing. His son, a major in the Air Force, told him stand-up was a military term and was created to bring together the key staff at the beginning of the duty day to share the important events affecting the unit. After a few weeks, he appreciated the concept behind the daily stand-up. Wolsey, a political appointee, had held several federal agency appointments in his career and most recently been police commissioner in New York City prior to coming to DHS.

Wolsey liked the morning stand-up. The briefing was a concise summary of key events affecting the security of the country during the past 24 hours, any new threat level intelligence, and major terrorist related events happening in the world. It also allowed him to pass on information or guidance to key staff members and respond to questions. The stand-up format eliminated the need for frequent formal meetings, which he avoided with a passion, and gave him time to pursue issues he thought were important to the agency. Wolsey signaled to the briefer to begin.

"Good morning, sir," said the briefer. "The key item this morning is the car bomb explosion at approximately 3:10 AM at the Grand City Mall in Cleveland, Ohio." Several photos of the crime scene were flashed onto the screen. "We have both FBI and ATF as well as local and state agencies on the scene. Other than the security cameras showing the car and an unidentified man running from the scene before the explosion, we have little new information."

"Any group taking credit for the explosion?" asked Hartley.

"No sir. All we know for sure is what I have briefed. It was agreed by the on scene responders that a joint federal-state task force be formed, with ATF assuming the lead at the crime scene. We hope to have more information by mid-morning."

"Did you pass this information to Director Bollino?" asked Wolsey.

"Yes sir. We sent a secure email to the White House situation room addressed to her for the meeting with the President this morning."

The briefer went on to discuss several continuing items of interest, as well as an update on the hotel bombings last month in Jakarta. As the briefer was concluding his presentation, the chief of current analysis, Richard Sandelman, asked a question about an ongoing intelligence report.

"Do we have any new information about that visiting professor in Vermont?"

"No sir, I don't," said the briefer, as he looked towards Doug Foreman, the chief of the preliminary inquiries branch.

"Dick, we sent a team of three people up there, but they haven't come up with anything yet." said Foreman. "They have only been there two weeks and have just established who the professor is and his daily routine."

Someone asked, "How long are they going to be there?"

"I don't know," said Foreman. "An allegation like this could take weeks or even months to resolve."

"What is this all about?" asked Wolsey.

Hartley pointed to Sandelman, who said, " A month ago we got a lead from the Egyptians that one of their citizens, a professor of Middle East history, was here on a two-year exchange program. The problem is he has a long relationship with a radical element of the Muslim Brotherhood. The Egyptians are convinced he also has a covert assignment for some possible operation against us or their Embassy here."

"How did he get admitted here, if he has terrorist ties?" asked Wolsey.

"He was sponsored through a program run by State, but this information didn't surface when our Embassy in Cairo ran checks on him."

"Great! So where is he now?" asked Wolsey.

"Dick's people gave us the intelligence report, and we found him at the University of Vermont in Burlington," said Foreman. "He teaches several classes a week and runs a seminar for graduate students in Middle East studies."

"Well, what is the game plan?" asked Wolsey.

"We're not sure yet," said Foreman. " We want to establish his routine to see what he does and whom he meets and then decide how to proceed from there."

"This could chew up a lot of time and people," said a senior analyst in Sandelman's branch.

"Sure, but we have to check it out," said Foreman.

"These people you sent up there, are they experienced?" asked someone. "If this guy is really here operationally, he could be trained and spot our people. Then what would we do?"

"Look," said Foreman, "we don't have lots of experienced people just sitting around here waiting to run down all the preliminary allegations coming into DHS. The people I sent up to Vermont are new, but they have been through training at FLETC (Federal Law Enforcement Training Center). I told them to keep a low profile while running down the leads and, if they have any situation arise where they could be compromised, to call me before proceeding. We are doing the best we can, with the resources Congress gave us." Foreman looked pissed.

"Doug," said Wolsey, "just calm down. No one is questioning your judgment. We have an experience problem in all the federal investigative agencies. The baby boomers are retiring and others are leaving for big money in private security. We just will work our way through this situation. The Director and I agreed to Scott Hartley's plan to put our most experienced people in the areas most likely for a terrorist attack. We are not alone. I was at a meeting recently where this topic was addressed, and the Bureau and every other agency is doing the same thing. We need to stress to our new people that they have an opportunity to take on serious responsibilities to protect our country, and we need to mentor and push ahead those people who show great promise."

Having given his unplanned pep talk, Wolsey looked around the room and said, "If there are no further comments, we stand adjourned; but give me any significant updates as they occur on the car bomb explosion at the Cleveland mall." With that, he and Hartley stood and left the room.

While the morning stand-up was taking place, the Director of DHS, Margaret Bollino, was over at the White House for an early morning meeting and photo-op with the President. Bollino was a career politician, having served as Governor of North Dakota and in the US Congress. She worked hard in her home state to get the President elected and was rewarded with the DHS position. She knew very little about security and thus let Wolsey run the day-to-day operations while she focused on the Washington political scene. He provided her talking points for her press briefings and, as long as she stayed to the script she was relatively safe from the media's probing questions.

CHAPTER TWO

It was two weeks after the explosion at the mall in Cleveland, Ohio, and morning prayers had just concluded at the Al-Mansur mosque in Newark, New Jersey. Aarif Sawalha was the Imam who conducted this morning's prayers, but Sheikh Al Sakhr was the leader of the mosque. Aarif departed the building quickly after prayers through a side entrance used only by staff. He walked through the alleyway connecting out onto Harrison Avenue and began a series of movements around Newark before catching the train for Penn Station in New York City. He had not detected any surveillance at the mosque or of him personally in the last week, but he knew the FBI had periodically been checking on the mosque.

There was a suspicion that the mosque's phones and mail were being monitored by federal agencies after the FBI had arrested a member of the mosque last year for soliciting money for a Yemeni charity. The FBI alleged the charity was a front for al Qaeda. Following the arrest, Aarif had a distant cousin rent a post office box for him at the main post office in Newark under the name of Josef Knowing. While Sheikh Al Sakhr was suspected of ties to radical Islamic groups, Aarif had kept a low profile from the police authorities and was very careful in discussions with fellow Muslims. Sheikh Al Sakhr's theory was that, if the American authorities could be convinced that he (Al Sakhr) was the person to target, then Aarif could be the contact with their brethren in the Middle East as well as moving about the United States. So far it appeared to be working; however, Aarif did not want any mistakes for the meeting today.

Aarif planned to spend two hours meandering along streets and visiting shops before he boarded the train at the

Broad Street station. The ride into the City was only twenty minutes or so, but he wanted to leave plenty of time to arrive at the meeting area. As he walked along the Newark streets, he rehearsed the arguments that he and the Sheikh had discussed last evening. While their plan was risky, they believed it was the best way to create apprehension and fear amongst Americans. They had plenty of money and had spent months carefully gathering small amounts of explosives to preclude notice by the ATF. Brothers from around the country had joyfully supported the effort without any idea as to where the material would go, how it would be used, or the timeframe. The best part of the plan was that just four or five trusted brothers knew of the connection with the Al-Mansur mosque, and only he and the Sheikh knew the entire plan.

Penn Station is located in midtown Manhattan between 7th and 8th Avenues. Aarif took the number 4 subway train uptown to E 72 Street. He departed the station, passed the building housing the Frick Collection on 5th Avenue, and entered Central Park. His destination was the area called the Sheep Meadow. The instructions were that, if the weather was good, this would the primary meet location; in case of rain, the alternate meet site would be the Metropolitan Museum of Art up by E 84th Street. Fortunately, this spring day was sunny and warm. This meant that many people would be out lounging on the grass or walking the paths crisscrossing the Meadow. The meet was scheduled between noon and 12:15 PM, a time when office workers would be crowding the park looking to get a start on their upcoming summer tans.

Aarif's instructions were to enter the park near the E 72nd Street entrance and walk south along the main pathway. He wore a plain brown suit, and white shirt with no tie. He had a Colorado Rockies baseball cap on his head and carried in his left hand a folded black umbrella that he used like a cane. The umbrella had a red cover with the word Coors in large black letters. The stranger that would approach him had been provided a photo of Aarif. The parole to establish their identity had to do with the umbrella and baseball cap. Aarif was told to walk south to where the path split off towards the Zoo. If no one had met him, he was to retrace his steps north towards the entrance he used coming into the park.

He proceeded along the pathway, trying hard not to look around but to blend in with the other noonday strollers. He worried about carrying an umbrella on a sunny day, but this was New York and the natives were used to bizarre behavior. When he reached the split for the Zoo, he turned around and began walking north. About 100 yards along the path, he saw a dark-skinned, middle-aged man sitting on a bench on the left side of the pathway. He had not noticed him on his way down the path. The man got up and started walking towards him. Aarif slowed his pace and prepared to stop.

"Excuse me," said the stranger, speaking Arabic, "Did you buy that umbrella here in New York?"

"No, I purchased it in Denver, along with my baseball hat, when I visited my cousin there," responded Aarif in Arabic.

"Mr. Sawalha?"

"Yes."

"You may call me Mr. Badami. Let us walk along back towards the Zoo. I know you do have a cousin in Denver, so if we are interrupted, I am a friend of your cousin and she asked me to look you up when I came to New York. Understand?"

"Yes, completely. How much time do we have?"

"I am a delegate to a sub-committee hearing of the UN Human Rights Commission, which is meeting here in New York in preparation for a full commission meeting in Geneva. We leave tomorrow, so I have this afternoon free. However, for our security we shouldn't tarry over our business. We understand you have a request for people?"

"Yes. We have a plan to help destabilize American trust in the ability of their government to protect them, but we need the right people to succeed."

"What is wrong with the American members of your group? Did we not spend time and money training them?"

"It is a cultural problem, Mr. Badami. These American jihadists are all talk when it comes to being martyrs. They will plant bombs in the middle of the night but have no stomach for self-sacrifice."

"I see. But you have no other way to implement your plan?"

"No. We need real Jihadists from the Middle East. Suicide bombings will unnerve the Americans. They have never known this kind of war except on television."

"How do you expect we would supply them? We just can't fly them into the United States like before. The authorities are wise to many of our past ways of bringing our people here."

"I know, Mr. Badami, but we must have them to succeed. We might lose a few brothers coming into the country, but if they don't know the plan before they get here, there will be no compromise. We know there are ways to sneak into the US. They already have millions of illegals here, and more come every day. The police agencies have their hands full and their politicians can't even agree on how to stop all the illegals."

"Where will you hide our brothers?"

"One of our trusted members has recruited a young American woman who has a farm house and barn in the country up north in the state of Maine."

"This American knows of your plans?"

"No, no! She doesn't know about the plan or us. She hates the federal government because they put her father in prison and took all the family money. It is a long story, but we are comfortable with using her."

"But how does that help you?"

"We will use her property to hide our brothers until we launch the plan."

"You can make your plan work by going to the country?"

"Yes. We must get our people out of the cities. The FBI is spying on us here in the large, metropolitan places. We worry about compromise. They will not know we have moved our fighters to the countryside. We have spent many, many hours studying this plan. It will work. We just need brothers to make jihad."

"Who will be in charge of this operation?"

"We have a young man, an engineer and a member of our mosque. He just completed training with our brothers in Pakistan. He and his family are reliable. He has befriended the American woman and believes he can control her. He also helped us develop the plan that you will review for us with the Council."

"Will this engineer be one of your martyrs?"

"No. We need his leadership for future operations. We also have an explosive technician whose work is reliable. He will prepare the necessary material for the jihadists. These two brothers are not expendable. If necessary, we will get rid of the woman once the operation is over. When we finish the first phase of this plan, we can move these two brothers to other places around the country."

"I will talk with the Council when I return home. Yes, we do have some people here who could help you bring in our brothers, but the Council must review your proposal. We don't want to risk exposing hidden assets on poor plans. Where and when will you want our brothers to travel?"

"I have all the details of the plan on this computer zip drive. I will give it to you, if you can get it through customs without compromise. "

"That is not a problem. I have access to the diplomatic pouch, and your zip drive will be as safe as if it were in my pocket. We do this all the time. Tell Sheikh Al Sakhr he will hear from the Council within a few weeks." With that, Mr. Badami shook hands with Aarif so he could take delivery of the zip drive and then headed for the exit to the park.

Aarif made his way back to Penn Station, timing his arrival about ten minutes before 3:00 PM. He made his way to one of the few public phones, which he had scouted out before leaving the station on his arrival. Precisely on the hour, he dialed a pre-arranged phone number to the main post office in Cleveland, Ohio. The phone was answered on the first ring.

"Teddy here," said the voice on the other end. This was the cover name for Ghanem, the technician. His real name before converting to Islam was Leroy Smith. He was a black American from Detroit who had adopted the single name Ghanem, which in Arabic means successful. He also had served a term in state prison for laundering drug money.

Without identifying himself, Aarif said, "Teddy, I hope you are healthy and all is going well?"

"I am fine and have no worries. I just hope to finish my work here soon and then come home. Do you have more assignments for me?"

"We will know about a new contract in a few weeks. Can you stay there until I have an answer?"

"No man, I am traveling home to see my gal. This place is boring."

"Okay, but start checking the web site in about ten days. When the new contract is signed, I'll have traveling instructions for you."

"Okay. I'll be waiting."

Teddy hung up, and Aarif looked around to see if anyone had been interested in his phone call. Seeing no one, he headed to the gate for his train to Newark. From the code words Ghanem had used, it appeared he was in no danger. He had gone to ground with a trusted brother who would keep him until he left for Detroit. Since he had never lived in Cleveland, there was little chance the police would be interested in him. Aarif thought Ghanem to be more a criminal than a committed member of the Muslim faith. However, despite his independent streak, he was an excellent bomb technician and enjoyed his work. They would have to watch him closely. In Aarif's opinion, Ghanem seemed to have few scruples, and there was always the possibility he could turn on them. But for now he was a critical part of their plan.

Aarif was confident that the Council would approve their operation, but would say nothing to Ghanem until they heard. Since he didn't fully trust him, he was concerned about leaks. Once the operation was approved, Aarif planned to send Ghanem instructions on how to drive to the location in Maine. Aarif would also travel north to tell Ghanem about the plan. He also wanted to make sure everything was being prepared correctly and tell Ben to watch carefully over Ghanem. Ben was a trusted brother but had no experience dealing with people like Ghanem. Since they could stand out as foreigners among the local Maine people, Aarif would have to outline how they were to act. He was also worried about having a woman, especially a non-Muslim woman, living amongst them.

CHAPTER THREE

Benjamin (called Ben) Panich climbed out of bed without waking the young woman sleeping next to him. He quietly walked out into the living room and opened the French doors leading to the patio. He liked the solitude of the early morning because it allowed him to think clearly without interruption. It was just about 5:00 AM. The springtime weather in Davis, California, was pleasing to him. The girl, Destiny Carter, rented this one bedroom garden apartment that looked out onto a tree lined bike path adjacent to a small park. It was only a ten-minute bike ride to the University where Destiny was pursuing a law degree.

He reflected on his homecoming last evening and decided it was good. Destiny was overjoyed to see him after a three-month absence. From their conversation and lovemaking last evening, he believed she had been faithful to him. While he was gone, she had been busy finishing up her spring semester courses and final exams. This was the end of her second year at law school. She had not really applied herself in undergraduate studies and admitted that law school was a challenge. However, she had become a "bookworm" this past semester so she would be competitive for work with a major law firm.

Ben had completed graduate studies in civil engineering last December but had remained at Davis after meeting Destiny. He was originally from New Jersey. His family, Bosnian Muslims, had emigrated from the former Yugoslavia and settled in New Jersey. When the troubles began in Sarajevo in 1991, his older brother went back to the family village to help fight the Serbs. Unfortunately, Ben's older brother as well as grandparents and other close family members were killed in the fighting. The TV scenes of

Muslim women raped and killed and thrown into mass graves had a dramatic influence on Ben. He blamed the West Europeans and the US for ignoring the carnage for almost four years before they acted. His growing hatred for the unjust treatment of Muslims led him to Sheikh Al Sakhr and finally to volunteer for the military training camps of Lashkar-e-Taiba in Kashmir, Pakistan. Ben had told Destiny he was going away for three months on a humanitarian project to help rebuild rural villages along the Afghanistan-Pakistan border. She thought that was cool but didn't seem surprised. He told her he would be back when she finished the semester and then they could go off together.

Ben and Destiny had met last year at a rally at the University. The rally had to do with the alleged atrocities committed by US troops in Iraq and Afghanistan. Following the rally, they began to meet and talk about their own experiences with the "imperialist west." Destiny was livid against what she called the "Feds" because of what they had done to her parents: her father had been convicted of drug trafficking and died in prison; the Feds confiscated the family's wealth, causing her mother to have a nervous breakdown. She died a broken woman. Destiny lived from hand to mouth until this past year when her grandmother died and left her a considerable amount of money and a farm in Maine. The grandmother had been estranged from Destiny's parents for a number of years because of their drug trafficking. Destiny had spent summers with her grandmother from the time she was young until finishing high school, but her mother refused to allow any contact after her father's criminal conviction. Her grandmother blamed Destiny's mother for getting her son involved in drugs. They had a terrible argument, and Destiny and her mother stayed in California until her mother's death. By then, Destiny was going to college in California and, for no particular reason, failed to re-establish a close relationship with her grandmother. She didn't even know her grandmother had died until a lawyer had contacted her about the inheritance. She blamed the Feds for all her family's troubles. However, the money from her grandmother's estate now allowed her to pursue law school. Her passion was to become an advocate for the poor and downtrodden who were, in her words, "held in slavery by the Feds."

While Ben professed affection for Destiny, he really saw her as an opportunity to further his goal to avenge his brother and their lost family members in Bosnia. While Ben was a committed Muslim, he did not follow all the prescribed rituals and practices. He did enjoy beer and wine, although he never drank around his family. In fact, he enjoyed most of the pleasures of Western society while professing hatred for their degenerate capitalist system. Intellectually, he understood this conflict between his religion and his own lifestyle, but rationalized his behavior as necessary to further the Muslim cause. His teachers in the training camp had told him that an Islamic warrior must often live a Western lifestyle in order to further the jihadist goals. However, in his heart he must remain loyal to the Prophet and his teachings.

Ben had told the Sheikh about Destiny earlier this year and proposed they use her as an unwitting accomplice in any plans to attack American targets. Ben believed that, while Destiny was a smart person, she was both naive about world politics and blinded by her hatred for federal authorities. The Sheikh had earlier confided to Ben that they needed to find a location to prepare an operation that was away from the city. Their group needed to keep the FBI focused on their activities around the mosque while they developed a covert capability somewhere out in the countryside. The problem was the group had no contacts in rural areas, and any overt interest by them would draw the attention of federal authorities. Perhaps Destiny could be the answer to the plans. So, over several months, Ben and a small cell from the mosque began to develop a plan to use Destiny and her farm in Maine. The problem now was Ben had to broach the proposal to her and get her agreement.

Destiny arose from bed about 7:30 AM and instantly smelled fresh brewed coffee. Ben must be in the kitchen, she thought. After her morning duties in the bathroom she went out into the kitchen. She saw fresh bagels and a container of her favorite veggie cream cheese spread on the table. "Hi," she said, as she put her arms around Ben, who was sitting at the table. "I see you have been to the bagel shop already; and fresh coffee and orange juice, too. What calls for this special occasion?" Ben believed the kitchen was woman's domain and that included shopping for food. She wondered what caused this new attitude. Was it the 3-month separation and their lovemaking last evening?

"Hi," he replied. "I was up early and couldn't sleep. I had a craving for bagels this morning and knew you wouldn't be up for a while. So, I went down and got this food so we could eat as soon as you awoke. Let's eat, I am famished."

"I guess from now on I'll only ask you to go to the store when you are hungry," she said.

While finishing breakfast, Destiny began to talk about possible plans for the day. She also asked Ben a number of questions about his trip and what the people were like. He told her a few things but decided he needed to bring up the house in Maine before they did anything else. He had carefully rehearsed what he wanted to say, and this was probably the best time for him to say it. Aarif had instructed him get Destiny's approval in steps to ensure they didn't compromise the plan if she were to object to any part of it.

She wasn't to ever know they were planning suicide bombings.

"Destiny, do you remember reading about the anti-Vietnam protests in the 1970's where the Weathermen bombed federal buildings?"

"Sure, I do. In fact Obama's friend, Bill Ayers, was one of them and now he is a college professor somewhere in Illinois. That must have been an exciting time to be on campus. I would have loved going after the Feds."

"Yes, it was exciting. Now, I have been thinking while I was away and have come up with a plan to start bombing federal buildings again. It would drive the Feds crazy and hopefully increase public support for getting the troops out of the Middle East. What we really want is to change people's opinion about Israel so our Palestinian brothers could regain their lost territory. If we keep the Americans busy with problems at home, the Feds won't be able to send troops back there to help Israel. Would you be interested in helping me and my friends?"

"That sounds exciting, Ben. But what would I do?"

"Now, Destiny, I am not just talking. Do you really want to be part of our group? It will be dangerous, and there is always the chance we could get caught."

"Ben, I'm becoming a lawyer to spend my life harassing the government and supporting the people against this corrupt system. If I get to blow up a few buildings, so be it."

He thought about her comments for a few seconds and decided she was really on board with him. She probably looked on it as an adventure. But, from their earlier discussions, he knew she really hated the Feds and, despite her intelligence, was very naive about world affairs. He decided to broach the next step.

"Ok, but this is real serious and you can't tell anyone. Agree?"

"Sure, I can keep a secret. What are we going to do, and what is my part? I don't know a damn thing about bombs or any of that stuff."

"Honey, you are going to play a key role by hiding and supporting us while we plan the operations."

"Ben, there's no room here to hide anything."

"Ah, but Destiny, you have a farm, and it would be the perfect place to hide while we get organized."

"You mean my grandmother's place in Maine?"

"Exactly. It's the perfect hideout. You showed me those photos. There is a large house and barns, lots of land and no neighbors."

"But, Ben, there aren't any really big federal facilities in Maine. There's just a little federal building in Portland. The rest of the state is rural. The best places to bomb are in the large cities."

"I know that, but we need a place to prepare, and then we will head out to the big cities like Boston and New York."

"But what do we need to do to get organized? Why can't we just organize in the cities?"

"I have been reading about the "cold war" terrorist groups: Bader Meinhof and all those groups. They made the mistake of organizing in the cities and universities where the Feds could infiltrate them with informants. The cities are where the Feds are well organized. No one would suspect we would be in a rural place like Maine preparing to blow up buildings."

"Ok, you convinced me. But what are we going to do in Maine to get prepared?"

"Destiny, first things first. Is it alright to use your place in Maine?"

"Sure, that's not a problem. By the way, how many people are we talking about, and how will we pay for all this? How will we hide people coming to a small town? It's not like Davis, you know. People will notice strangers and ask questions."

"Okay. Let's go slow here and I'll fill you in on the plan. If we can use the place in Maine, I have friends who have money and will support us. I also met some guys in Afghanistan who will help us. They are coming to the states anyway and don't like the American government for what they have done to their villages. I also have a couple of friends here who will help us."

"Gosh, Ben, you have been planning this for a while haven't you?"'

"You gave me the idea, Destiny, when we were doing those protest rallies last fall. Remember what you told me what happened to your Dad and Mom? I then started thinking about it while I was gone and also talked to some friends.

But, Destiny, you are the key to our planning, and I wouldn't want to do it without you. We really are an ideal couple."

"Oh Ben." She got up, went around the table, and hugged him. "Let's go back to bed," she whispered, "and you can tell me all about what we are going to do."

CHAPTER FOUR

It was late in the afternoon in Washington, DC. It was about a month or so after the mall bombing in Ohio. Scott Hartley knocked on the open door of Deputy Director Wolsey and walked into his office. "I got your message, Bill, that you wanted to see me."

"Good news, Scott. The Director called me on her way to Andrews Air Force Base. She has just finished meeting with Senator Lovingman, and he likes our idea of contracting with some experienced people to help us when we have an overload of work.

"Well, with the support of the Chairman of the Homeland Security committee, we should be able to start right away. Are there any restrictions?"

"No. The President has talked with the Congressional leaders of both parties and everyone seems to be on board. No politician wants to be caught hindering our gains against terrorists; especially if we have productive leads we can't get to."

"The Director said we should start with a few contracts using people who are well known to us. They will have to be folks who have worked for the government in the past and have security clearances. Other than that, we are free to use our own discretion. Have you talked with The Berwick Group?"

"I had lunch with Nola Hunter yesterday, and we were able to agree to a contract. She is just waiting to hear from us. She and Patrick Draper have been taking it easy lately, so they are ready to jump in again."

"Has their business been slow? I know several DC investigative firms have laid off people due to the recession."

"No. They have plenty of work, but they have been sitting back and giving it all to their staff. In fact, Patrick is up in Maine fly-fishing. I spoke with him this morning, and he was happy to go over to Burlington as soon as the contract is signed."

"So, Patrick will work with the lads checking on the Egyptian. What are the ground rules?"

"I talked with Ken Booth. He's the team chief up there. I told him that he was in charge, but that they should use Draper as a valued advisor. I told Draper the same thing. Both of them know that the key to this thing is cooperation. None of our people up there have ever worked against a foreign operative. In fact, they all have little surveillance experience. I told Booth that Patrick not only has years of experience but has worked with young agents when he was running the Air Force Office of Special Investigations."

"So, we have to worry most about our people listening to an outsider and being prepared to 'take a hit' if things go wrong?"

"I don't think it will get to that, Bill. Patrick isn't looking for glory, and he told me he will consider the job a success if he can make the team look good."

"Scott, I'll rely on you to watch this on a daily basis. You know many of our senior people are dead set against bringing in outside consultants for operational work, so this will be the test. If Patrick works out well with the Burlington team, we can do more of these operations. But if it blows up, the nay-sayers will never let us forget it."

"I know, Bill. We have hashed it to death here, and the rules of engagement are clear. But, like all good ideas, they can get ruined by people getting into 'pissing contests. I'll watch it closely and keep you up to speed."

"By the way, what will Nola be doing here at the headquarters?"

"She and Patrick will initially work for me in the Special Analysis Center (SAC). The SAC will be a new branch directly under me. That's where we will house the consultants until we feel comfortable with this program. Nola will be working primarily with our new analysts. You know that analysis was an FBI weakness prior to 9/11, and Nola was one of the few I could go to over there. She was great at reading the reports and then connecting the dots. That's what we need here, and it takes time to develop a good analyst."

"Well, that shouldn't raise a lot of controversy. It's the operators here that are doing all the griping."

"Not necessarily, Bill. Dick Sandelman is saying that Nola will be interfering in his business. Sandelman especially has raised arguments about outsiders. He is a good manager but has strong opinions about everything. I know there is strong professional jealously between him and Nola from their FBI days. Supervisors want to train their own analysts and won't like Nola looking over their shoulder. But they don't have the time to train and manage too. I have told everyone we are going to work as a team, and, if there are issues, we will sit together and work them out."

"Scott, while I approved the concept, I can see where Doug Foreman will be uneasy, since the three guys in

Vermont work for him and Draper will be under your wing, so to speak."

"Doug and I have discussed this, Bill. I told him we would work together as we smooth out the rough edges of this arrangement. Once you feel comfortable with the process, I'll have Foreman supervise Draper. I eventually would like to use the SAC branch as an administrative place to house consultants, and then parcel them out to offices here and operations in the field as needed."

"It should be lots of fun here the next few months," said Wolsey. "I don't mind professional disagreements as long as they are focused on identifying terrorists and preventing attacks. I'll also say a few comments to the senior staff before Nola arrives. They need to know that, while this is a test program, it has Presidential and Congressional support. We screw this up, and it could affect staff and funding, let alone protecting our country. By the way, do you have any plans for Nola to be out in the field?"

"I may send Nola out to help us with an assignment occasionally, but basically we can best use her here at Headquarters. She doesn't like to travel too much, anyway. Being a widow, she has the two kids to take care of along with her mother."

"What happened to her husband?"

"He also was an FBI agent. He got killed when a crazed druggie ran into a police precinct in the District and started shooting up the place. They killed the druggie, but not before he had shot several cops and Nola's husband: a real tragic affair. She took early retirement to take care of the kids. A couple years later, she teamed up with Patrick, and they started The Berwick Group. They lined up jobs with a couple of large K street law firms here, and the business took off."

"Bill, you mentioned Director Bollino going out to Andrews AFB. I thought she was leaving for the terrorist conference in Belgium later this week."

"She decided to leave early and visit her counterparts in Germany and France before the conference starts. She has all the talking papers and possible Q&As that your people wrote for her, so she should be okay."

"Well, as long as she stays on script, she won't make any headlines. I hope she has learned her lesson from her previous trip, where the reporters knew more about the subject than she did."

"I think she will do well, Scott. She knows she has little experience in this business, and if she keeps to the talking points she won't get into trouble."

"Well, I guess it could be worse. Fortunately, she is staying out of our operations."

"Scott, between us, her forte is making announcements that make the President look good on homeland security. Other than that, she knows nothing about our business. But she is a fast learner and will work hard to stay out of trouble and not embarrass the President."

"Well, at least she knows her limitations. I'll keep a close watch on our operation in Burlington. If we can get this advisor concept to work, I plan to use it on a couple more operations. By the way, there is nothing new on the bombing in Cleveland. There have been a few crank messages, but no credible group has taken responsibility for the bomb.

Neither the Bureau nor the ATF have any good leads, so we may be at a dead end."

"Will there be any political fallout if we don't come up with a suspect?"

"Not right away. We're putting out the usual announcements about following up on leads, and we are lucky that the female security guard is recovering from her wounds. If anyone had died, I'm sure we would be getting more pressure from the politicians and the media."

"Okay, Scott. I'm leaving early. I am the stand-in for the Director at the Japanese Embassy reception tonight. If you need me, I'll have my secure phone."

"Well, Bill, someone has to do the party circuit, and I'm glad it's not me. See you tomorrow."

CHAPTER FIVE

Ben and Destiny stepped off the plane at Newark International Airport and headed for the baggage claim area. Unknown to Destiny, he had arranged for a brother from the mosque to meet him, but first he had to get her settled. He had told her little of how they were going to get to Maine except that they would drive from New Jersey. She hadn't asked about where they would get a car, and he decided to say as little as possible. Fortunately, their baggage was on the carousel when they arrived.

"Destiny, why don't you take the shuttle over to the Marriott and get us registered. I need to get us a car, and I'll meet you over there in a little while."

"Okay, but where are you going?"

"I just have to meet a friend, and he is going to give us a car to use while we are here on the East coast. I won't be long, and we'll eat dinner at the hotel when I get back."

She seemed to accept his direction without any trouble, so, while she headed for the hotel shuttle, he walked outside and headed over to the passenger pick up area. He had sent his plane schedule to Aarif so they could meet him. After a few minutes of searching the passing vehicles, a black Toyota Highlander pulled up and, while he didn't recognize the driver, he saw Aarif in the rear seat. He put his bags in the back of the SUV and got in the rear seat with Aarif. They greeted each other warmly, and the driver pulled away from the curb, heading for the airport exit. Aarif introduced him to the driver and told Ben it was okay to talk about the project.

"Good trip, my brother?"

"Yes, Aarif. No problems. I sent Destiny to the hotel and told her I would join her shortly."

"I won't keep you long, Ben, but there are a few changes. We are heading out of the airport to get the car we have for you, but I wanted to talk with you without the woman around."

"Is there a problem?"

"No, but I am going to ride up north with you tomorrow."

"Do you think that it is wise for Destiny to see you?"

"We won't worry about that now. You just introduce me as Josef Knowing, and I am a friend from your old neighborhood who is helping with the project. You can tell her I am the money man, but nothing else."

"But why are you coming with us?"

"I need to be there when Ghanem shows up. I sent him a message and he should get there in a few days. I need to set him straight that you are in charge. You and I also need to talk about how you will handle him. We can do that after we get up there. I'll just tell you now that, while he is a good technician, I am not convinced we can fully trust him. He converted to Islam while in prison, and I'm not sure if he is working with us because he is a true believer, or if he is just interested in the excitement of the project. Despite his young age, he was a career criminal before he came to us. We need to make sure he will follow our direction and not go off and compromise us and the project."

"I thought our brothers in Detroit fully vetted him."

"They did before they sent him to the training camp, and he excelled there. But he wasn't brought up like you. He was a member of the Ummah in Detroit. This is a group of black men who converted to Islam, most of them while they were in prison. They profess Islam, but have a history of violence. Ghanem separated from the Ummah after the group had a shoot-out with the police. He joined a mosque in Detroit, and our brothers spotted him because of his professed commitment to Jihad."

"What does he know about our project?"

"He knows nothing yet, except that I want him up in Maine to do a job for us. We will tell him some of the details after he arrives, but not everything-especially the targets. We had him do a test with a car bomb at the mall in Cleveland to be sure he learned his lessons well at the training camp."

"That was his work I saw on TV?"

"Yes. He did a good job, and the police have no clues that it was he, since he is really a guy from Detroit. Don't worry, Ben. I'm just being careful. We have much riding on this project."

"I also think it would be wise for me to be there when our brothers from outside the US arrive. We don't know who they are and what they know about the United States. We may have to do some adjusting to our plan based on what we see. I have discussed this with Sheikh Al Sakhr, and he fully agrees. I am to be the go-between, so, if there is any compromise, I will be the fall guy, so to speak. We must protect Al Sakhr and the mosque from this operation."

"This is getting more complicated than we thought, isn't it, Aarif?"

"Don't worry, Ben, we will go forward one step at a time. If we are careful, Allah will guide us."

"Aarif, I need to tell you about Destiny, so you won't be shocked when you meet her tomorrow."

"I understand she is not one of us, Ben, and I am used to seeing women parade around Newark like common sluts."

"Aarif, Destiny is a beautiful woman and she dresses to show off her body and good looks. She also is an independent woman who believes in women's rights. In California, she would be called a 'free spirit'. I took her shopping before we flew out here and told her she needed to buy some clothes that covered more of her body. She got upset, but I told her she would be working with some of our friends who were conservative Muslims."

"And what did she say to that? Is there a problem?"

"I don't think so. At first she was mad and said she wasn't going to cover up like the women at the mosque. She was ranting about women having to wear the niqab and all that stuff. But she finally calmed down, and I got her focused on what we are going to do. Although she is a smart woman, she is blinded by her hatred for the Federal government. We need to play on that factor. That's why I tell her as little as possible about our operation. She is somewhat naïve about world events and doesn't pay much attention to them, so that's good for us."

"Well, we don't want her walking around dressed like our women. It would draw too much attention to our project. Just emphasize to her that she should wear conservative dress, and there won't be any problem."

"Okay Aarif, but I'm telling you all this because she will freely state her opinion and not in the least be intimated by you. You will have to be careful how you react to her."

They drove into a small shopping mall and parked next to an identical SUV. Aarif handed Ben the keys and told him this was their car for the journey. The vehicle had a Florida registration and license plates. "Tell Destiny the car belongs to a friend who doesn't need it this summer," said Aarif. "I read that many people come to Maine in the summer from Florida, so the car should not stand out."

They agreed to meet at the Marriott in the morning for breakfast, so Ben could introduce Destiny to Josef Knowing before they left for Maine.

CHAPTER SIX

Patrick left from his home in Bath, Maine shortly after 8:00 AM and planned to be in Burlington, Vermont, by mid-afternoon. There was no rush, and it was a beautiful spring day. He had read again the bio's on the team in Burlington. Ken Booth had been appointed the team chief because he had been a cop for ten years in New York City with the NYPD. The other two members, Albert Young and Bruce Thompson, had no investigative experience before coming to DHS. Young had been in the Army Special Forces for five years, and Thompson was in the Virginia National Guard, and both had served a tour in Iraq. Booth was married to a female police officer in the NYPD, but the other two guys were single. Scott Hartley told him that Booth was an experienced cop, who was a team player and eager to sharpen his skills as an investigator. Booth didn't carry a grudge about federal law enforcement officers like so many local cops who had a bad experience with "the Feds." He accepted the fact that some people just acted stupid because they were impressed with their position.

He had rehearsed what he planned to say to the team and was happy that these men were mature and had real world experiences. Too many of the people coming into the federal investigative agencies today were bright college grads but had little "street" experience. He also knew that Scott Hartley had a lot riding on this advisor concept to make up for the lack of experience by all the new troops. Most all the senior operational types at DHS had opposed Hartley, and it was only the support of Bill Wolsey that allowed this test to go forward. Patrick and Nola had discussed this project at length, because they had their reputation to consider and the effect the results would have on their business. The Berwick Group was in good financial shape at present, but it wouldn't take much to send clients scurrying off to another investigative firm. And if the project were successful, they could rely on future contracts.

Patrick had arranged to meet with the team at 4:00 PM at their team house. They picked that time since the team was busy on surveillance during the early afternoon. Because the students from the University of Vermont were finishing up the spring semester, there were apartments for rent for the summer. The team had found a small house and leased it for two months. Patrick decided to take a room at a hotel, since he wouldn't be there full time and it gave him some space to supervise his Berwick work. He also planned to talk with Ken Booth about bringing up Berwick's Tech guy, John Carver, who would be a valuable addition to the team. Carver had been a career Army member and served with the Special Forces. So far as Patrick knew, the DHS team had been using physical surveillance to watch the Egyptian, and he thought it was time to introduce modern electronic measures into the operation.

A six-foot tall, middle-age looking guy answered the door. He had a thick crop of sandy hair, a light complexion, and a face and eyes that were serious but not threatening. He was dressed in casual sport clothes that helped him fit in with the college scene, maybe as a college employee or a professor one would see on the streets in Burlington. He had a slight paunch but was not overweight. When Patrick had talked with him on the phone, he detected a slight New York accent but it wasn't so pronounced that he would stand out in Burlington. Fortunately, the city population came from everywhere because of the colleges in Burlington.

"Hi, I'm Patrick Draper."

"Ken Booth," he said. "Glad to meet you after our telephone talks. Come on in and meet the other guys."

Patrick followed Booth into a living room that was decorated in what one would call early fraternity house décor. "Don't mind the furniture," Booth said. "We didn't have a lot of time to go house hunting and this place is well situated for our work. We can actually walk to our posts from here."

The two other fellows in the room got up from a couch. "Hey guys, this is Patrick Draper. Patrick, meet Al Young and Bruce Thompson. They shook hands, and Young said, " I understand you are a retired General. I was a sergeant in the Army. What do I call you?"

"How about I call you Al and you call me Patrick?"

"That's fine with me." He smiled. "I just wanted to get that straight since I've never worked with a General before."

Young looked to be about 5'10" tall, with the build of a fellow who obviously worked out in the gym. He had short, dark hair, piercing brown eyes, but a warm smile. He could be called handsome and had a rugged outdoor appearance that surely attracted the many young women who saw him on the streets of Burlington. He was young enough to fit into the campus scene, possibly as a graduate student; in fact, he was taking night classes back in Oregon to complete his degree. Young had completed three years of college but had run out of money, so he enlisted in the Army with the idea of finishing his education later. About a year ago, he became engaged to a hometown girl back in Oregon, and that was his reason for leaving the Army. Patrick's first impression of him was that of self-confidence but not a big ego type.

Thompson had the build of a basketball player, which he had been at the University of Virginia. He appeared to be about 6'4" tall without an ounce of fat on him. He was a good-looking guy with ebony skin, expressive dark eyes, and a warm smile. Patrick thought the college women here would go for him as he walked around the campus. On finishing college, he had worked for a brokerage firm until his National Guard unit was sent to Iraq. Upon returning to the United States, he decided to join a federal investigative agency for the experience. His long-term goal was to complete law school and go into politics. He was a man with an infectious smile and Patrick immediately felt he would be a good team member.

"I understand we can learn a lot from you, Patrick", said Thompson, "so I'm really glad you are here. All of us got good training at the Federal Law Enforcement Training Center, but we sure could use some street experience from an on-scene advisor."

"Well, thanks for the compliment, Bruce. You guys are just as smart as me. My advantage is I have worked these kind of targets for more years than I want to remember; so I'm just here to lend my experience and help you guys be successful."

"Patrick," said Booth, "why don't we talk about how we are going to work together, and then we can fill you in on the target."

"Good idea," said Patrick. "Let me tell you what Scott Hartley outlined to me, and then we can discuss it and get all the questions out of the way."

"How about we have a beer while we're talking?" said Young.

Booth went to the kitchen and came back with a 12 pack from a local micro brew and some peanuts. They all took seats and Patrick began his spiel.

"Okay, this is your first assignment as DHS investigators, and you're involved in a covert surveillance of a person who is alleged to be a terrorist or have terrorist connections. You have been trained to do this work, and I am sure you can do it well. My role is to lend my experience to help you do your job. We'll talk over what you need to do, how you can do it, and I'll make suggestions and comments. I am not in charge here. Ken is the team chief. Any questions so far?"

"Yes," said Thompson. "What happens if we want to go one way and you say no way, who decides?"

"Good question," said Patrick. "When we work as a team, everyone has input, so that we have looked at all the options before we move. Many times, there are a variety of ways to do something, and, after we have discussed it, Ken makes the decision."

"Okay," said Young. "I like that method, but what if Ken makes a decision that you think will compromise the case. What do we do then?"

"Patrick and I have discussed this very point on the phone yesterday," said Booth. "We will strive to work so that we don't get into that position, but, if it happens, he and I will get on the phone with Bob Hartley, tell him our issue, and work it out with him. By the way, Hartley agrees with this idea."

Both Young and Thompson nodded their heads in agreement. Thompson said, "I like that idea, because if we screw this up, all of us are going to take a hit, not just Ken. Isn't that right, Patrick?"

"You are on target, Bruce," Patrick said. "Remember, we can all be in agreement on some action and still mess it up. So we want to work together. I have as much riding on this case as you do, and my goal is to have you three be successful, whatever the outcome."

They spent the next hour working out a lot of minor details and questions and finally agreed they had a good plan for working together. Patrick looked at the clock and said, "How about we order in pizza, my treat, and then you guys can brief me on what you have done, what the target is doing, and what we need to do next?"

Everyone nodded yes, and Young jumped up and went to the phone to order the pizza and some more beer.

CHAPTER SEVEN

Aarif was waiting in the lobby of the Marriott when Ben and Destiny came down for breakfast. Ben introduced Aarif as his friend, Josef Knowing. Destiny was her usual warm, smiley self and put out her hand to Aarif. He hesitated and then put out his hand to hers. Ben didn't think Destiny noticed the hesitation, since Aarif avoided physical contact with women other than his family. However, he did notice Aarif closely checking out Destiny and her clothes. Actually, Destiny was dressed conservatively, wearing dark slacks, a white blouse, and a dark green cashmere sweater draped over her shoulders. She looked great and smelled great, too.

"Ben tells me you are going to stay with us in Maine," she said.

"Yes, that is correct," said Aarif. "I want to help Ben with getting our project organized, so I'll just intrude on your hospitality for a few weeks, and then I must be back here for business."

"Oh, what is your business, Mr. Knowing?" said Destiny.

Aarif was taken back, since he hadn't anticipated the question. In fact, he was not accustomed to women speaking to him unless he asked them a question or gave an order. Therefore, he hadn't prepared any cover background except his statement that he was a friend of Ben.

Ben jumped in before Aarif started stammering and said, "Josef is a financier for many of our friends who are in business."

"Yes, that is correct," said Aarif.

"So you are a banker?" said Destiny.

"Not quite like you think of a banker, Destiny," said Ben. "Amongst our people, we use wealthy men like Josef to conduct business, since many banks hesitate to loan us money. It is an old custom amongst Islamic people. Many of our people feel more comfortable doing business with Josef and avoid bankers and their high interest rates." With that, Ben pointed Destiny and Aarif towards the dining room and hoped he could steer the conversation onto safer grounds, since Aarif wasn't prepared for a conversation with an American woman, especially someone like Destiny. She might be naïve, but she had a way of drawing people out in conversation.

They were seated by the hostess and began looking at the menus she gave them. She poured coffee for them and said that a waitress would be over in a few minutes to take their order. Ben noticed that Aarif kept making quick glances at Destiny. While he professed to stay clear of Western women and their provocative dress and manners, he seemed to be intrigued with Destiny. From conversations with Aarif and bits of information he had learned at their mosque, he knew that Aarif was about 40 years old and not married. He came from a family in Egypt that had long ties with the Muslim Brotherhood. Aarif mentioned once that he had been to jihad training camps in the frontier area of Pakistan and had fought with the Taliban in Afghanistan against the Russians before the Americans invaded the country. Supposedly, Aarif had come to the U.S. on a student visa, but Ben wasn't quite clear how Aarif managed to stay in the country.

Looking up from her menu, Destiny gave Aarif a smile and said, "Would you mind if I called you Josef? I do hope you will call me Destiny."

Aarif gave a furtive look towards Ben and said, "If you insist, Ms. Carter, I mean Destiny," he stammered. He was obviously uncomfortable, since, in his normal day-to-day activities, he never really engaged Western women in conversation, let alone found himself sitting next to one who wasn't wearing some fashion of Islamic dress.

Destiny winked at Ben and then turned towards Aarif. "I hope my dress doesn't make you uncomfortable, Josef. Ben tells me that you are not used to women wearing Western clothes. I will try to be conservative in my dress, but there is no way I am putting on one of those nigab dresses that covers one head to foot."

"No, no, I understand, Ms. Carter, I mean Destiny," said Aarif. "I understand we come from a different cultural perspective, and I don't mean to impose my values on you."

"Well, I hope you find my values acceptable, Josef," said Destiny. "My friends would certainly wonder about me if I suddenly showed up in Maine in Islamic dress."

Ben stayed clear of the conversation but was prepared to jump in if Aarif should become flustered. He thought that Destiny was still a bit peeved about their discussion on dress back in California, and was making a point with Aarif that she didn't plan to conform to their standards of dress. While Aarif wasn't used to dealing with Western women, he wasn't stupid and would placate Destiny in order to complete the project. Besides, Aarif would get his revenge if he decided that Destiny was of no use after they finished their work. Ben hoped that he could get Aarif to see the long-term benefit of using Destiny for future projects, but that all depended on how she reacted when the real targets were made known. Ben enjoyed Destiny and their sex life, but he had no long-lasting feelings for her.

"Oh, I didn't mean to offend you," said Aarif. "I sometimes choose the wrong word since English is not my native language. I fully understand you must conform to your culture, and we don't want anyone in Maine to start asking questions about our project."

Aarif looked to Ben for help with the conversation, but fortunately the waitress appeared to take their order.

CHAPTER EIGHT

As they finished eating their pizza and beer, Ken brought out a small stack of photos. "This is our target, Patrick," he said, as he showed him the first photo. "His name is Dr. Akil Hakimi, professor of ancient Middle East history. He is 45 years old and here on a two-year exchange program. He taught two undergraduate classes this semester and a graduate seminar. He will be teaching a graduate seminar this summer and, as far as we know, has no plans to go home to Egypt on vacation."

Dr. Hakimi had the dark skin pallor of a Middle Easterner. His hair was black with a sprinkle of grey, and he was developing a middle-age paunch around his waist. He had dark eyes, and his demeanor did not appear inviting from the photo Patrick studied. Ken said he was about 5' 9" tall and always dressed in Western clothes, usually with an open-collar dress shirt and either a suit or sport jacket with khakis or jeans.

Bruce said, "For a guy who is only here for a couple of years, you would think he'd travel around and see the sights. But, as far as we can tell, he just goes from home to the campus and sits at the coffee place downtown."

"Does he have a daily routine?" Patrick asked.

"He sure does," said Ken. "He is like a machine. Every afternoon, rain or shine, he goes to Java Joe's, a coffee place on the walking mall in the center of Burlington. He arrives at 2:00 PM, stays for an hour, and then leaves. He buys one cup of coffee and reads his newspaper. We think it is an Egyptian paper from home that he gets in the mail, since we never see him go to the newspaper store on the walking mall."

"First, we thought he was going there to look at the women," said Al Young. "The place is always crowded with college students and young professional people. But he doesn't girl or boy watch. He just drinks his coffee while he reads the paper and then leaves."

"Have you ever seen any of his students approach him?" Patrick asked.

"No," said Ken. "We haven't seen anyone talk to him. Java Joe's has tables and chairs in front of their place and he sits outside in good weather and inside when it rains."

"Maybe he just likes Java Joe's coffee," Patrick said.

"We have thought that, too," said Bruce. "He doesn't have any family here, and maybe he's lonely."

"Where does he live?" Patrick asked.

"That's the interesting part," said Ken. "He is living in a large house, that belongs to another professor who is overseas on a sabbatical. The house is on a cul-de-sac, so we can't do any surveillance there. We would love to know if people are visiting and who they are."

"Well," said Patrick, "if he is trained in clandestine tradecraft, he has picked the right place to live. Do you know if anyone else is living there?"

"We don't think so," said Ken, "but we can't really tell, since we can't watch the place. So far, we haven't seen him with anyone else. Bruce follows him often on campus and, aside from passing the time of day with people, he is always alone."

"When we first got up here, school was still in session, so I audited one of his introductory classes one day," said Bruce. " It was one of those large theater lecture halls and he doesn't take attendance, so there wasn't a problem. He speaks English very well and used a lot of photos and vugraphs. He also used humor to keep the lecture lively. A few students stopped him after class to ask questions, but I didn't see anything unusual."

"Do you think he would recognize you if he saw you in town?" Patrick asked.

"No, I was just another pretty face in the crowd," said Bruce.

"Who knows that we are here?" asked Patrick.

"I took care of the liaison," said Ken. "We briefed the local police chief and the FBI Resident Agent. The chief got us a room over a restaurant on the walking mall, where we have a direct line of sight to Java Joe's. The restaurant owner is a woman who is friends with the chief, and she thinks were here on narcotics surveillance. She has teenage kids and doesn't like drugs, so she is very supportive. The chief has used her in the past and says she'll keep her mouth shut. The FBI RA is undermanned and overworked and told us to keep him in the loop if we need help. In fact, he introduced me to the police chief."

"We decided not to brief the campus police," said Al. "Most all of our work is in town, and anyone can walk on campus. Ken has us rotating our posts, and, with all the people in the walking mall, it's easy to blend into the crowd. If

Dr. Hakimi is teaching class, he walks from the campus to Java Joe's. Then he goes back to the campus parking lot and drives home. If he is off that day or if it is a weekend, he drives to the mall, finds a parking place, and walks over to Java Joe's. When his time is up he gets back in his car and drives home."

"I have us using three positions," said Ken. "One in the room over the restaurant with a camera; one of us nearby in the walking mall; and one in a car, in case we need to move out quickly. This has worked out fine, and we haven't lost him yet."

"That's interesting that he goes to Java Joe's on days when he doesn't have class," said Patrick. "Does he have any other routines that you've noticed?"

"Other than going to the grocery store and dry cleaners on occasion, he doesn't do much travelling," said Bruce. "That's why I said before I find it strange he doesn't go sightseeing or take trips over to New York State, or even Canada, since the border is so close."

"Well, Patrick, what do you think?" said Ken."

"I think his behavior is strange, but then we don't know much about him or his circumstances. I want to think about this overnight. If you guys don't have any objection, I am going to bring up my tech man, John Glover. He can set up a remote camera in the room over the restaurant and help us with the surveillance. That will also free up another person for street work. Ken, if you could get the names of the people who live on the cul-de-sac and run a little background check on them, we might be able to set up a remote camera targeting Hakimi's house."

"That's no problem getting the names, Patrick. The records are public, and I'm sure the police chief will assist us with the background checks. I also like your idea of some technical help. Why don't we meet for lunch tomorrow, and we'll trade ideas on where to go from here."

CHAPTER NINE

Melissa Wallis, the supervisor on the night shift at the DHS Operations Center, was having coffee and a sweet roll at the small snack bar in the headquarters building. She normally was home in bed by now, but monthly she attended a supervisor's meeting held right after the morning stand-up briefing. The meeting is chaired by the Ops. Chief, Scott Hartley, and usually lasts less than one hour. This morning's stand-up was running late, and she thought the snack and coffee would keep her awake through the meeting and the ride home.

A woman, unknown to Melissa, approached her table and said, "Hi, my name is Nola Hunter. May I join you, the other tables seem taken?"

"Please do," she said. "I'm Melissa Wallis, the night supervisor in the OC. I heard your name and understand that Scott Hartley is going to introduce you at the supervisor's meeting this morning. So it's good to meet you before the formal meeting."

Nola placed her tray on the table and took a seat across from Melissa. "Thank you, Melissa. I hope the meeting goes well, since I know some of the supervisors are against bringing in an outsider to train new analysts. I used to be with the FBI, so I don't usually consider myself an outsider."

"Well, you won't get any argument from me. I welcome anybody who can improve our threat analysis program. I know we are hiring three new analysts this month, who just graduated from college. I read their resumes. All are very bright, educated young people, but have no real-world experience. Two of these kids never even had a part-time job! I run the 10 PM to 6 AM shift, so I'm sure at least one of them will end up with me."

"I see you are married. Does the night shift work out OK for you?"

"Right now, it's fine. My husband is an attorney over at Justice. We have three kids, two boys and a girl. My husband gets them up, and I get home to feed them breakfast and send them off to school. Then I sleep and wake up in time for the kids' arrival home. We all have dinner together, and then Karl, my husband, takes over until they go to bed. Another year or so, and my colleague on the day shift is going to retire, and Scott tells me I can move to days."

"I know the difficulty about scheduling work and children, especially since I lost my husband. Fortunately, my mother lives with us, so she is always there if I have to travel."

"I remember reading about that shooting in the DC police station several years ago. It must have been awful for you. I know Karl considered the FBI at one time but then was offered a position at Justice."

"We always knew the risk of both of us being FBI agents, but you never think it will happen to you. Fortunately, Patrick Draper came along with the idea of starting The Berwick Group, and that has been a life saver for me."

"Well, The Berwick Group sure has a great reputation around this town, so I'm glad it worked out for you."

"Melissa, I just hope this training idea works out, or the reputation of The Berwick Group could go into the toilet."

"Don't worry, Nola. I think the biggest complainer is Dick Sandelman, and everyone here knows he doesn't accept change easily. He's also a bit of an MCP and likes to rule the roost."

"I knew Dick from my Bureau days. We never worked together but were in headquarters at the same time. I think he believed that I got the job of public affairs officer because my husband was close with the former Director. What Dick didn't know was that I was in the media business before becoming an FBI agent."

"From talking to colleagues at my level, I think they will welcome you, Nola, and any help you can give us. We get inundated at times with information, and having people who can pick out the nuggets from the chaff is our major need. Some of our senior people have forgotten how difficult it can be working in the trenches, so to speak. "

"Melissa, every federal agency seems to have an experience problem. It's the baby boom generation retiring. Patrick and I have offered our services and will do our best to make this work."

About that time, the doors to the senior conference room opened. "Well, stand-up is finally over, so we can go in now. Good luck, Nola," said Melissa.

CHAPTER TEN

The drive to Maine was relatively uneventful. Ben and Aarif sat in the front, and Destiny occupied the rear seat. She listened to her iPod and observed the scenery because it had been many years since she had driven from New York to Maine. She did begin to wonder how all this was going to work out. How many people were coming to the farm; who was going to take care of them; how would she explain all these strange people, especially strangers like Josef, who spoke broken English. The more she thought about these things she decided to start making a list of questions to ask Ben and Josef.

The men were speaking what she thought was Arabic, which surprised Destiny, since she never knew that Ben spoke that language. She wondered if they were making plans that they didn't want her to know about, and if this was going to be the norm while they were in Maine. Finally, in frustration, she said, "Hey, what are you guys talking about that you don't want me to understand?"

"Oh sorry," said Ben. "I was just filling in Josef about your place in Maine, and we just sort of lapsed into Arabic. It was a good way for me to practice the language, since I don't often get a chance to speak it that much anymore. We didn't mean to slight you."

"It was my fault," said Aarif. "Destiny, you interrupted at a good time, because, other than seeing photographs, I don't think Ben knows too much about where we are going and what is there. I have many questions, so perhaps you could give me the 'big picture,' so to speak, if that is the right phrase to use."

"Okay. Let me give you the history of our farm and what it is like today," said Destiny. "In fact, I don't think Ben and I have ever talked about the history of the place, which is very interesting."

"We have several more hours to drive, so give us the whole picture," said Ben.

"The farm has been in my father's family since the early 1800s. Originally, it was just a small place with crops, a few cattle, and some lumbering. My great-grandfather enlarged the place by buying property from neighbors and got into the dairy business. With the enlarged property came a nice trout stream and a big pond. In all, we own about 500 acres."

"Do you still have cows?" asked Aarif.

"No, my grandfather, who was a stock broker, turned it into what we would call a *gentleman's farm* today. There are no animals, or crops or anything else. There are large fields, and twice a summer a farmer comes and cuts the grass for hay for his animals."

"Will they be cutting grass when we are there?" asked Aarif.

"I don't think so. We had a late spring, and they usually cut grass in early July. But I'll check with Mr. Hartwell, who is the estate manager for me."

"Hartwell doesn't live there, does he?" said Ben.

"No, no one lives there. Mr. Hartwell lives in town and hires people to take care of the place, and I pay him for that service."

"Will people be coming out to the farm all the time?" asked Aarif.

"No", said Destiny. " I called Mr. Hartwell and told him we would be there for several weeks and would take care of the place. I also said that Ben was working on his thesis for a masters degree, and I had a lot of studying to do for the bar exam next year; therefore, we came up here for peace and quiet and did not want people out there disturbing us. He said he understood, and for me to just call him when we were leaving."

"How about other people visiting?" said Ben. "You must have old friends from when you spent summers there."

"I think most of them have moved on to other places, but I will use the same story I gave to Mr. Hartwell if I run into people I know. I will have to visit Paine's Corner. The Paine family runs a large grocery store, and gas station at an intersection in town that is named after them. The family has been there for generations, and their daughter Ginny and I were best friends during my summer visits. Mrs. Paine runs the grocery store, and her husband has the gas station and repair garage. So I will need to visit them."

"Will they want to visit out at the farm?" asked Ben.

"I hope not, but let me think about that problem," said Destiny. "Besides, we are going to have to buy groceries from Paine's while we are here. However, when Josef's people arrive, someone is going to need to drive into Portland to do the big shopping for food and things. We can't be buying food for all these people at Paine's and pretend we are just two people living on the farm."

Aarif looked at Ben with a worried expression. It was dawning on him that there were numerous logistical and other issues that they had not considered, especially when moving into a rural community. In fact, all that Aarif had known since coming to America was big cities, where people could easily get lost in the crowd. He had no experience living in the countryside, especially in this place called Maine.

"Now, I have some questions for you guys," said Destiny. "How many people are we going to have out at the farm, and who is going to take care of them?"

"We are not sure," said Aarif. "We have a technician who is arriving in two days, and I hope to have five drivers individually arrive during the next two weeks; but I don't have the schedule yet. Can your house hold that many people?"

"Rooms are not a problem," said Destiny. "The original farm house has been modernized and has three bedrooms. The house sits on the original stone foundation and looks rustic from the outside, but it has all the modern conveniences we need and use today. A breezeway connects the main house to what is now a guesthouse, which my great-grandfather built as a bunkhouse when it was a working farm. This house has also been renovated and has its own kitchen, dining room, and big family room, along with a master bedroom and about ten small bedrooms. He used it for the hired farm hands, but it has been used for summer guests since my grandparents owned the place. So there is plenty of room. But who is going to cook and clean for all your people?"

Both Aarif and Ben looked at each other with startled expressions: another logistical problem that they had not considered. In their culture, these domestic issues were women's work, and so they had never thought about such matters when planning their operation. It also dawned on Ben that Destiny wasn't going to be their housekeeper. While he had a fleeting thought when they were planning this operation to ask Destiny if she knew how to cook, it now seemed apparent to him that she had no plans to do any of the women's work while they were at the farm.

"From your silence, I can see you hadn't considered that issue," said Destiny. "For the record, I am not the cook and housekeeper. I also don't know what kind of foods your guests will eat, so someone who knows their dietary requirements will need to do the shopping."

"We will figure this out," said Ben. "Just give us a day or so to find someone to come up here."

Aarif placed his head in his hands and rocked slowly to and fro. What would he say to Sheikh Al Sakhr when he sent him an email this evening? The Mosque had more domestic help than necessary, and he was sure someone could be sent up here, but this lapse in planning did not look good for him. He needed to focus on the operation and didn't need all these domestic distractions. The Imam might wonder what other things he had not considered in his planning. This Destiny might prove more of a problem than a blessing. He thought her attitude was typical of these young sluts strutting around the city, thinking they were so much better than others. A proper Muslim woman would be proud to serve them and gladly die to further their cause. After several deep breaths, he calmed himself and prayed. Aarif believed that Allah, who is so great, would show him how to prevail against these blasted infidels. For now, he had to hide his disgust and work with this bitch of a woman. After several moments of quiet prayer, he said, "I will arrange for someone to be here within two days, if that is not a problem? She will take care of all the domestic chores, the cooking and cleaning and whatever else needs to be done. If you could just accompany Ben, he will do all the shopping at the store in Portland."

"I guess I can help Ben," said Destiny, "as long as he has money to buy what we need. For the next couple days, I'll get some prepared meals, and we can use the oven or microwave." She wasn't excited about domestic chores and wanted this Josef to understand she wasn't going to be a house slave for these guys. She caught him staring at her at the hotel and thought he was creepy. Destiny wondered if she had made a mistake letting these people use her farm. However, it would only be for a few weeks, and, as long as she hung out with Ben, she believed she would be okay. Besides, she was looking forward to some rest, and summer at the farm was always a treat.

They stopped north of Hartford for lunch and then continued on the interstate into Massachusetts. Destiny had been listening to her iPod and dozing off and on until they crossed the Piscataqua River from New Hampshire into Maine and headed north on the Maine Turnpike. She had thought of suggesting they stop at the New Hampshire liquor store before entering Maine, but decided that would probably get Josef all excited. She wondered what his reaction would be when she broke out the wine for dinner. It should be an interesting few weeks, she thought, as she smiled and looked forward to teasing creepy Josef. Destiny believed, from the responses to her questions, that Josef and Ben had not thought a bit about feeding and housing their people- unless they mistakenly thought she would do all the work. She realized that Josef was a real MCP when it came to interacting with women and wondered if Ben might also have some of those tendencies which up until now he had been able to hide from her. She liked Ben a lot, but perhaps it was time to look elsewhere for a mate. The last thing she wanted was to be trapped in the culture lived by Josef. The more she thought about her situation, she realized the next few weeks would be a good test of what life would be like with Ben and his family.

As they neared the town of Saco, she directed Ben off the highway and to a shopping center with a Hannaford's grocery store. She had Ben accompany her into the store so they could purchase a few items for the morning's breakfast. They took a grocery cart and began strolling along, looking for the items on the list that Destiny had prepared while riding in the car. "When we leave here, I want you to drive west on Route 5, and I'll direct you to the various roads that will take us near Paine's Corner and the farm," said Destiny.

"Where are we going to eat dinner?" asked Ben.

"I want to get to the farm while it is still light, so I can find the key and get the main house open. Mr. Hartwell said that the electricity and everything would be ready for us. I don't think much has changed in the house, but I just think it is easier to get our bearings while we have the daylight. Then we can drive back down towards Portland and find a place for dinner."

"That makes sense to me," said Ben.

"I suppose we'll have to give Josef a bedroom in the main house, but I really would like to send him to the guest house."

"I know he appears different, Destiny, but he means well. He was brought up in a different culture and is not used to being around women in such close quarters. This project means a lot to him, and he really appreciates you lending us the farm."

"Well, he has a funny way of expressing his thanks. I also am sure he had some notion that I was going to do all the housework until I set him straight. You need to tell him, Ben, that I want to be treated like a princess while we are here. I'm sure that will frost him, but he needs to know us American girls are raised differently than what he experiences in his own culture."

"Oh, don't get upset, Destiny. Josef will be okay, and this project will be over in a few weeks, and then we can possibly go on a little vacation up here."

"Ben, I am on vacation right now, and don't you or Josef and whatever people are coming here forget it." She smiled and blinked her eyelashes at Ben. They finished the shopping, and, after Ben paid the bill, they headed back to the car.

CHAPTER ELEVEN

Burlington is a lovely city in the late spring. The weather was sunny and warm with puffy clouds this day, and a light breeze came off lake Champlain, cooling the many runners moving along the lakefront pathway. There were sunbathers, too, using their lunch break to get a head start on their season's tan. There were also the usual gawkers checking out the females who were sunbathing. Patrick and Ken Booth sat on a wooden bench eating sub sandwiches and drinking beverages they purchased from a cart vendor on the lakefront.

"I had no problem getting the names and backgrounds of the residents who live around the professor on the cul-de-sac. It seems most of them are employed at the University, but only a few are long- time residents of Burlington," said Ken.

"That was fast work. You must have developed good relations with the police chief."

"I think he likes me because we approached him when we first got to town and haven't played any games on him with regard to our activities."

"Well, I drove around the cul-de-sac this morning," said Patrick. "I figured, with my Maine license plates, I could explain being lost. However, I didn't see a soul on the street. I did pick out a house that is directly across from the professor and would make an ideal spot for a camera covering his house. Who do you have living at number 46 Ward Circle?"

"That would be Dr. Nancy McCray. She is a professor at the medical school, owns the house and has lived there for over 10 years. I think she may be single, approximately 45 years old, and is registered as a Democrat on the voting rolls. I couldn't find anyone else residing at that residence. The police chief doesn't know her, and a check of the NCIC and local police files was negative."

"How about the residents on either side of her?"

"Well, one is also a professor at the University in the history department. Unfortunately, the police chief knows who he is because he has been involved in numerous anti-establishment marches in town. The chief wouldn't recommend approaching him. The neighbor on the other side of Dr. McCray is an engineering professor but is away until next fall. The chief knew that information because the house is empty while the guy and his family are away, and the police periodically check the house for him."

"Unfortunately, we will need access to the interior of a house to set up our concealed camera position. Let me talk with my partner, Nola Hunter, and see when she can come up to help us. I think an approach to Dr. McCray with a female as the lead interviewer may be the best way to assess her."

"Since we don't know much about her, how will you make a decision on asking her help? She could be one of those wild college liberals who doesn't like the police!"

"Well," said Patrick, "we will probably have to wing it, but I'll check with Scott Hartley before we do anything. Normally, what we do is to engage the person, telling them that we are involved in a national security matter and are trying to determine facts. We ask the person if they wouldn't mind signing a non-disclosure agreement before we discuss any details. Depending on how the person reacts, we act accordingly. Medical doctors are usually stable individuals, and, if Dr. McCray has any objections, she probably will be up-front with us. The non-disclosure agreement has some very heavy language about criminal penalties, which is helpful, too."

"Patrick, do you really think a concealed camera will be that much help?"

"It's a crapshoot, Ken. The camera records motion and will give us 24-hour coverage of the house. We can set up our monitoring station either at your place or a van, or both, which gives us advance warning when the target is moving. It also will give us coverage of someone visiting the professor. John Carver is a pro at this stuff, and I defer to his judgment on how he will set up the system. I'm not a tech. person but I do know what technology can do for us. He also will provide us camera coverage of Java Joe's so no one has to sit up in the room across from the target. We never know what the results will be, but, if we have activity, I always like to have documentation."

"Sounds good, Patrick. When will I hear from you?"

"I'll talk with Scott and then call Nola. She might be able to do this as a day trip, depending on the airline schedules. Nola will call Dr. McCray from DC and tell her she wants to make an appointment for us to fly up here to see her and that it involves a confidential matter. That usually piques peoples' attention and gets us in the door pretty quickly. Of course, if we get the cold shoulder, we will have to go to plan B, whatever that will be."

Ken laughed and said, "Do we need to do anything else up here while you set up the interview?"

"No, just keep an eye on the professor. Depending on when Nola can get here, I may go back to Maine but am available on my cell phone. If I stay here, I can pull a shift with you on the afternoon surveillance. I've never had Java Joe's coffee. I'll call you when I know the schedule."

With that, both men got up and strolled from the lakefront to the parking lot. As he drove away, Ken reflected on the lunch meeting. It had been productive for him to learn how one goes about mapping out a strategy to move the case along. He was also interested in how they would use the camera system. He had no idea how long this surveillance would go on but thought that, with Patrick assisting them, there would be more activity than just watching the professor at Java Joe's.

CHAPTER TWELVE

After breakfast at the farm, Destiny gave Ben and Aarif a tour of the property. She had shown them last evening how to activate the alarm systems. There was one for the main house and guesthouse, as well as an alarm signal about 100 feet along the driveway, that sounded in the kitchen when any vehicle approached the house. There also was a gate that could be closed to keep vehicles from approaching the house. The gate was located about 200 feet past the alarm signal, where the blacktop pavement began. The gate could be opened and closed electronically from the house, and there was a speaker system that allowed them to talk with visitors before the gate was opened. They decided, for security purposes, that they would use this gate while they were here to prevent anyone from unexpectedly coming into the property.

The buildings were not visible from the main road because there was a stand of trees that were approximately 200 feet in depth from the main road into the property. It was almost 500 feet from the main road to the farmhouse. A few years ago, the county mandated that all these long driveway roads needed to have a name posted on a pole where the driveway intersected the main road. This was so emergency vehicles could find the address. Her grandmother named the driveway Carter Lane, but didn't pave the first 200 feet to give the impression this was just an old dirt road. The rest of the drive was blacktopped several years ago to make it much easier for snow removal.

She had arranged with Mr. Hartwell to have both houses cleaned before their arrival. She hoped that when they inspected the guesthouse Aarif would express an interest in staying there. No such luck! He liked the guesthouse and even the décor in the individual bedrooms, all of which had their own bathroom. He even expressed amazement at the modern kitchen and the comfort of the great room; unfortunately, he had staked out a bedroom in the main house with a view of the driveway and demonstrated no intention of moving.

At breakfast, Aarif informed her and Ben that a woman was arriving tomorrow from New Jersey to take up all the cleaning and cooking chores. He didn't say how he had arranged this housekeeper so quickly, but did say she was very trustworthy and would be no problem for their project. Destiny had asked Aarif what manner of dress she would wear, since Destiny was sure this woman was someone from Aarif's culture. He said she would be dressed conservatively but not wear any female Muslim clothing. They would have to meet her flight at the Portland airport and transport her to the farm. She noticed that Aarif had been a bit less condescending this morning and wondered if Ben had talked with him.

Both Ben and Aarif were impressed with the size of the two barns located about 300 feet to the rear and to the right side of the guesthouse. One barn was two stories high with a large loft. The apparatus for the milking cows had long ago been removed and sold. The second barn had once held the farm machinery, but all that was left now was a mid-size truck that was used to plow snow and a few other lawn machines. This barn also had a workshop for repairs of equipment and other projects. In addition to the barns, there was a three-car garage that included her grandmother's GMC SUV. Mr. Hartwell said the car was currently registered, and he had Paine's garage tune it up so Destiny could use it. The garage was off to the left side of the main house. A circular driveway looped around the front door of the main house, passed the garage area, and continued out to the main road.

Ben and Aarif decided that the technician would work in the old cow barn, since there was plenty of room to park and set up the vehicles for the project. Aarif also informed Destiny that the technician would be arriving tomorrow, too. He would be driving a car, and she and Ben would have to meet him at a designated location and lead him to the farm.

"How about meeting him and picking up the housekeeper at the airport in the same trip? Then we can all go to the grocery store in Portland before returning here," said Destiny.

"We can do that," said Ben. "Where shall we meet the technician?"

"I was given the name of the *Books a Million* bookstore in the Maine Mall, before we left New Jersey," said Aarif. "That will be the meeting place."

"The Maine Mall is right off the turnpike," said Destiny. "If he gets off at that exit and parks in front of the *Books a Million* bookstore, which is a separate building, we can meet him there. How will we know who to meet?"

"I am the only person who knows him, so I should go with you," said Aarif. "He is a black American and will be driving a car with Michigan license plates."

"That fine," said Ben. "However, we don't need five people to go grocery shopping."

"Ben, just you, I, and the housekeeper will go into the grocery," said Destiny. "Josef and the technician can stay out in the other car. We need her to figure out what to buy for this crowd. Plus she has to cook what is bought. By the way, Josef, what is the housekeeper's name?"

"Her name is Nasheed, which in English means *Beautiful One*."

"Well, I hope she isn't too beautiful, given that you are bringing all these men in here," said Destiny.

"She is married, very discreet, and there will be no problem," said Aarif. "She has worked at our local mosque for several years and we consider her to be most reliable."

"And how do we address the technician?" asked Destiny.

"He uses the name Ghanem now," said Aarif. "He used to have an American name but goes by his Muslim name now. In English, Ghanem means *Successful*."

"Well, that's what we want him to be," said Ben.

"Josef, do all these people understand they are going to remain hidden on the farm while they are here?"

"Yes, Destiny," said Aarif. "Everyone coming here knows how important this project is to our group and will obey my instructions."

"Well, the reason I ask is, since this Ghanem fellow is an American, he may think he can move around here freely and go into town. This is a rural area, and strangers hanging around here will be spotted rapidly. I don't want anything to spoil my reputation here or any scandal involving the farm."

"Destiny, Josef and I have discussed the danger of operating out here away from a big city. The men coming here know security is critical, and Josef plans to reinforce the rules repeatedly while we are here."

"Okay, Ben," said Destiny. "Just remember, people here think it is only me and a boyfriend, so let's not have anything happen to ruin that story."

She walked them away from the house and barns and strolled out along a dirt road that led to the fields of pasture. The grass was getting up near the calf of her legs and it would soon be time for the first cutting. However, she was certain they would all be gone before the farmer arrived with his machinery. She showed them the pond, currently occupied by a pair of mallard ducks, and the stream off in the distance that flowed through the property.

"I need to go to Paine's Corner this morning," said Destiny. "The Paines know I am here, and so it would be expected for me to stop at the store to say hello and buy groceries. I'll leave you two to look over the place some more and plan how you can get this project done quickly. I'll be back by lunchtime."

As she walked away, she detected by his expression that Josef wasn't used to a woman telling him what to do and making decisions for him. She thought maybe the next few weeks could be a lot of fun.

CHAPTER THIRTEEN

Destiny pulled into the parking lot at Paine's Grocery and entered the store. A customer had just finished checking out and was leaving the store. Mrs. Paine looked up over her glasses to see Destiny.

"Well, aren't you a sight for sore eyes," said Mrs. Paine. "John Hartwell told us you were coming back this summer, and now you're here. Destiny, you look great, that California weather agrees with you. Wait till I tell Ginny you're back. She asks me every day if I have seen you. Come on over here so I can give you a big hug."

"It really is good to be back, Mrs. Paine. I was so sad that I didn't get to see Grans before she passed away. It was a tough time trying to mediate between my mother and Grans. I sure miss them both."

"Your Grans passed away suddenly. She was here one day shopping and looked fine. The next day, they were rushing her to Maine Medical Center, but it was too late. She died on the way. By the time John Hartwell was able to find you, the funeral was over."

"I know. He was very apologetic when he finally located me. When mom died, I moved to Davis and was living in a graduate apartment just off campus. That's why no one knew where I was living. But that's all in the past, and we have to move on with our life."

"Well, are you here to relax for the summer?" asked Mrs. Paine.

"Not really. My boyfriend, his name is Ben. We came up here for some quiet, get-away time, so we can complete some serious studying. Ben is working on a master's thesis, and I am trying to get ahead of my studies and prepare to take the Bar exam next year. So we won't be doing much socializing."

"Well, you sure will have some time to visit with Ginny and her young baby. I don't know if you were aware that she married Tom Longley. It will be two years this August. They have a little boy, named Thomas, and of course we all love him."

"No. I didn't hear any of that news; that is very cool. I'll have to give her a call this week and stop by and see her. I'm not sure I know Tom Longley."

"They met at the University. Ginny went to U Maine at Orono, and she met Tom, who is from Cumberland. They knew each other for a couple of years but didn't get serious until their senior year. We really like him. Remember our son, Glen? Well, he is living in DC. He's in training with the State Department: going to be a diplomat. So it's good to have an adult young man around here. We have our hands full taking care of the garage and store, and we aren't getting any younger."

"That is great news about Glen. I guess those four years at Georgetown really paid off for him. How did you get so lucky to have Ginny and her family living here?"

"Tom is a State Policeman and was fortunate to get assigned in this area. We know he'll have to move at some point, but it is wonderful to have them here now while the baby is so young."

"If you give me Ginny's phone number, I'll call her this week and stop by and see her once I get settled. It will be fun to re-connect with her. She was my best friend when I spent summers here, and I have great memories of this place because of that. Oh, I also need to buy some groceries this morning."

Destiny grabbed a cart and worked her way around the store, getting enough groceries for two people. She figured that she would need to continue to shop at Paine's for her and Ben so no one would be suspicious. When she went to check out, Mrs. Paine gave her Ginny's telephone number and address.

"Ginny and Tom live only 15 minutes from here," said Mrs. Paine. "They were able to buy a cute house in a new development, which makes it easy for Ginny to come by and help out when it is busy on weekends. She brings the baby, and of course our customers love to see and talk with the baby. Tom works a lot of shift work, so coming down here helps to pass the time; and, best of all, we get to see our grand baby."

Both women hugged as Destiny got ready to leave the store, and she promised to bring Ben by so Mrs. Paine could meet him. A young boy who was stacking cans in an aisle in the front of the store helped her out with the groceries. Destiny wanted to go over to the garage on the way out and see Mr. Paine. He had always been so kind to her and her mom, and she really enjoyed his Maine stories. She would have to hurry, though, so the ice cream would not melt.

CHAPTER FOURTEEN

After talking with Nola, Patrick decided to stay in Burlington. Scott Hartley agreed with him about approaching Dr. McCray, and Nola said she would call her that afternoon. Nola called back in the late afternoon and said she talked with Dr. McCray, who agreed to meet with them. Unfortunately, she only had some free time Friday about 11:00 AM.

After checking airline schedules and appointments, they agreed that Nola would fly up late Thursday afternoon so they could make the meeting, and then she could fly back to DC Friday afternoon. They also decided to bring up John Carver with his van and tech gear, since they wanted to be ready if Dr. McCray agreed to work with them. They were going to set up a camera system, anyway, to keep track of Dr. Hakimi for his daily visits to Java Joe's.

❧

Meanwhile, in Maine, Aarif had made contact via the Internet with the brother who was to bring in the explosive material for use by Ghanem. Ben and Aarif had scouted the area in their SUV while Destiny had gone to the store. There seemed to be more traffic in the daytime than they had experienced arriving last evening. It was now daylight saving time, and it didn't get dark in Maine until after 8:00 PM. They decided that the best time for the truck to arrive would be early evening, just as it was getting dark. The traffic should be light, and, using GPS, the driver should be able to locate and enter the property without looking around. The last thing they wanted was a lost driver asking for directions. The plan was for the driver to arrive and back the truck into the cow barn. They would unload the truck and send the driver and truck away to Portland, where he could spend the night before traveling back home.

The truck and driver were coming from a town south of Chicago. The explosive materials had been gathered from around the country in small quantities, some of it being stolen. Neither Aarif nor Ben had any knowledge of explosives and were relying on Ghanem and the brothers gathering the materials to know what they were doing. There were also five suicide vests coming with the explosives.

The driver estimated that he would arrive on Saturday or Sunday evening. He was the only one to whom Aarif had given the exact address of the farm. Aarif did not want the driver waiting around somewhere for Ben to meet him, with the chance of coming under suspicion by the police. He wanted the explosives delivery to be quick and then send the driver and truck away from the farm.

The cars to be used in the operation would come from different States. Brothers, who had no information about the project, would deliver the cars to the Portland area and be met by Ben and Destiny. They would take the drivers to the bus station or airport and then return to the meeting point to pick up the extra car and drive it to the farm. For security reasons, Aarif wanted the cars to arrive at the farm near darkness. Aarif would need to have Ben speak with Destiny to get her to agree to help with bringing cars to the farm. When possible, he did not want to deal with her, because he had never been around such a strong willed-woman. In his opinion, these American women were wild and degenerate and needed a strong man to tame them.

The question now for Aarif was when the Jihadists would arrive. He didn't want them here too early, but he wasn't sure how much control he would have on their travel. He needed to train them for their mission and how to get to their respective destinations. He had maps and routes for them to take, as well as stopping places along the way. This shouldn't take long to do, but each driver would need a back up plan in case of problems. Once they drove away from here, they would be on their own.

There was to be no communication that could tie them to either the farm or the mosque in New Jersey. In fact, the directions for the journey would start with leaving Maine on the Turnpike. He wanted them to leave here near darkness and have Ben lead them to the Maine Turnpike. By arriving and leaving the farm during darkness, he didn't think any of these men would remember how to return here.

Aarif's other concern was the men having too much idle time and being around Destiny. She was dressing somewhat conservatively for an American, but her movement and actions were provocative. She was a good-looking woman and would certainly draw the attention of the men. He didn't know what previous experiences the men would have had with Western women, especially pushy women like Destiny. There wasn't a lot to occupy their time here except for television, which was also scandalous for religious Muslims. Perhaps he could have Ben find some appropriate books at the store in the Maine Mall.

The more Aarif contemplated the problem of keeping the men busy, he decided they would spend their time in the guesthouse and not wander into the main house. Fortunately, the housekeeper Nasheed was near 50 years old and had children who were in their twenties. Although she had been pretty as a young woman, she had experienced a hard life here.

She had married young and her husband had decided for them to live with his mother. It had not been pleasant, and Nasheed was at the beck and call of her mother-in-law, a tyrannical old crone who treated her daughter-in-law like a house slave. A few years ago, Nasheed began to volunteer some time at the mosque in order to get out of the house. She was a good worker and very discreet about what she saw and heard at the mosque. When the mother-in-law died three years ago, Nasheed was offered a full-time position, which her husband fully supported. He liked to brag that his wife was the senior assistant to the Imam. Since she had two sons, she might have some ideas on keeping the men occupied and calm.

CHAPTER FIFTEEN

Patrick met Nola at the Burlington International Airport. She had taken a direct US Airways Express flight from Washington Regan Airport, arriving close to 5:00 PM. It had given her most of the day to work at the office and to bring along a number of items she needed to discuss with Patrick concerning their Berwick Group business as well as her training sessions at DHS.

"Nola, you're just in time for cocktails," said Patrick as he gave her a hug. "Let me take your bag and head out here to the parking lot. I've got you registered at the Marriott, and we are scheduled to have dinner with the DHS team at 7:00 PM."

"As usual, you have everything arranged," she said. "I really enjoyed the view as we came into the Burlington area. This is pretty country, and I don't think I've been up here before. It must be nice to live in a small city with lakefront views. "

"We will have some time in the morning for me to show you around before our meeting with Dr. McCray. One thinks of cows and farming when they mention Vermont. However, Burlington is a sophisticated but liberal college town, which my native Vermont friends say is not the real Vermont. Meanwhile, let's get you settled and then have a drink before we meet the guys."

"Suits me. I haven't been out to dinner or drinks for weeks, so I'm ready to see the town."

The team gathered at Isabel's Restaurant on the waterfront. Patrick introduced the team members to Nola. Ken Booth had selected the restaurant because of the views of Lake Champlain and the quiet atmosphere. He had requested a table that would allow them privacy-not that they were going to talk a lot about the project, but Ken was a careful guy when it came to security.

"This is a delightful place," said Nola. "Do you eat here often?"

"First time for us," said Al Young. "We're usually pizza and beer guys watching sports on TV."

"Don't let him kid you, Nola," said Bruce Thompson. "We do get out to dinner often, since there are so many good restaurants here and the prices are good. But we hadn't been to Isabel's before."

They ordered drinks, the team drinking beer and Patrick and Nola trying a bottle of chardonnay recommended by the waiter. Everyone was hungry, so they got the food selection out of the way when the waiter returned with the drink order.

"If you have time, Nola, there are pleasant sightseeing cruises on Lake Champlain," said Bruce. "We took the *Spirit of Ethan Allen II* last Sunday. It was an interesting cruise, because they have a narrator who points out all the important sights around the lake."

"I would like to do that, Bruce, but I'm only going to be here until tomorrow afternoon. I have a late afternoon flight back to DC, so there won't be much time for sightseeing. Patrick is going to drive me around a bit in the morning before our appointment."

"Well, maybe on another visit," said Ken. "We would like you to come by and see our observation post before you return."

"I would like to do that," said Nola. "I also want to take a stroll along the pedestrian mall. A friend told me I should do that and have a cup of coffee at Java Joe's." Everyone smiled at that remark, and Nola winked back at them.

CHAPTER SIXTEEN

Destiny returned from Paine's Corner with groceries. She had purchased a selection of cheeses and cold meats at Paine's so they could make their own sandwiches for lunch, as well as some frozen dinners. She noticed that Aarif didn't seem to be overly excited about making his own sandwich, but she was determined not to be a waitress for him.

Ben and Aarif spent the rest of the afternoon discussing their plans, while Destiny lounged outside on the porch reading a Jodi Picoult romance novel. She enjoyed relaxing, since this was the first break she has had since her law exams. She wondered what kind of peace and quiet she would have when all of Josef's friends showed up-especially if they were all like him. There was a gazebo on the other side of the pond, and, the more she thought about it, she decided to set up lounge chairs and a table out there. It would be her refuge when she needed to get away to sun bathe and read. She could also take a swim in the pond, which was fed by the stream that crossed the property.

At breakfast the next morning, Destiny asked, "What time to we need to be in Portland today?"

"Nasheed's flight arrives at the Portland airport at 4:45 this afternoon," said Aarif. "I told Ghanem to meet us in front of the bookstore in the mall at 6:00 PM."

"If her flight is on time, we may be able to do the grocery shopping before we meet this guy," said Destiny. "I hope you told her to prepare a list, so we don't spend all night in the grocery store."

Aarif look annoyed. Who was this woman to be giving him orders? But he swallowed his pride and only said that she would have a list of things to buy.

They drove into the Portland Jetport about 15 minutes before the plane was to arrive. Ben and Aarif went into the terminal to meet the plane. Destiny pulled into the parking area, where she could wait as long as she stayed with the car. She knew it would be a while, so she was glad to have her novel to read.

Ben had asked her earlier if she would help him gather the men and cars that would be coming to Maine. She had agreed, but now thought it would be a couple of weeks of waiting around to meet these people. Just like they say in the Army, she thought, *hurry up and wait.* This was not the adventure she had envisioned when Ben asked about using the farm. It appeared now there was going to be a lot of boring waiting and dealing with straight-laced people like Aarif. She was determined she would not take any guff from them.

Aarif spotted Nasheed as she and other passengers exited the arrival area on the second floor of the terminal. He introduced Ben to her, and they headed for the baggage claim area. Aarif began immediately speaking to her in Arabic, and, from what Ben could pick up, he was giving her instructions. He heard him say that she must always call him Josef and that she was not to tell the American woman anything about their activities at the mosque in New Jersey. She continued to nod her head and agreed with him.

The wait for the baggage was long, but this gave Aarif time to repeat all his instructions to Nasheed. While other passengers were enjoying meeting friends and relatives, Aarif continued to drone on with his orders for the poor housekeeper. Her bag finally arrived on the carousel, and they walked out to the parking area to find Destiny.

Destiny spotted them and honked the horn. She then got out of the car and posed to meet Nasheed. The woman was dressed conservatively, with a headscarf. She was tall, and had a very pretty and soft face, with dark black eyes that set off her light complexion. Destiny had pictured a short, stocky Middle East female with dark complexion, but Nasheed didn't fit that image.

"Hi there," she said. "My name is Destiny, and I'm pleased to meet you. Josef hasn't told me much about you, except that you are going to take care of his friends for a couple of weeks."

"Yes, I am here to do the housekeeping and pleased to meet you, too. Do I call you Destiny?"

"Yes, please do, and would you mind if I call you Nasheed? It is a pretty name, and Josef never told us your family name."

"Oh, yes, call me Nasheed, everyone does. I have never been up here in the North, so I am looking forward to my stay with you. Josef says you have a big farm out in the country."

From first impression, Destiny thought she would get along well with Nasheed. She felt sorry that this woman would be tasked with so much cleaning and cooking and have to put up with the arrogance of Josef. However, she would not get involved. If she lifted a finger to help, Josef would try to start bossing her around, too.

"We need to go to the grocery store, and there is one adjacent to the Maine Mall," said Destiny. "Why don't we leave you off at the bookstore, Josef, and you can browse for books you want to take out to the farm while you are waiting for your guy."

Josef gave her a dirty look but didn't disagree. They headed out from the airport for the short drive to the Maine Mall. "I thought we would be in the country, but this mall looks like the malls we have in New Jersey," said Nasheed.

"Oh, we will be in the country soon," said Destiny, "but this is a good place to shop. In fact, it is the only mall we have in this part of Maine, and it probably has all the stores you have in New Jersey. Today we are going to that large supermarket over there, but perhaps one day we both can come down to the mall and shop."

"I would like that," said Nasheed.

Destiny pulled up in front of the bookstore but didn't park the car. "Okay, Josef, you can go find books, and we will drive over there to the grocery store. We should be back in a half hour or so and will meet you here."

Aarif just looked at Destiny but didn't say anything. As he got out of the car, he stopped and said, "Be back here by 6:00 PM," slammed the door, and walked into the store.

CHAPTER SEVENTEEN

Nola and Patrick were directed by a security guard to the office of Dr. McCray at the medical school administration building of the University. However, they were surprised to see a temporary placard on the office door that stated she was the acting Dean of the school. They entered and found this was not the ordinary office of a professor. It was apparently the Dean's office that she now occupied. A secretary greeted them and said that Dr. McCray would be with them as soon as she finished with a phone call.

As they started to take a seat, the inner office door opened, and a woman walked out into the outer office. She approached them and reached out to shake hands. "Ms. Hunter, Mr. Draper," they both nodded yes, "I am Nancy McCray. Pleased to meet you."

"The pleasure is ours," said Nola, "and we appreciate you making time for us today."

"Please come into my office," she said. "These are only my temporary digs while our Dean, Dr. Morrow, is on sabbatical. Come August, I go back into my humble office down the hall."

Patrick observed that she certainly didn't look her age. He estimated she was about 5'6", trim figure, with short blond hair and no make up. She had a pretty face: thin, with almost no wrinkles, hazel eyes, a small mouth, and seemed to smile easily. Like a man, he wondered why a good-looking woman like her wasn't married. She was dressed in a running suit with sneakers. As they walked into the office, she directed them to a corner where three soft, cushioned chairs surrounded a small coffee table. "Please excuse my casual dress. I have a busy day, but wanted to fit in a run between our appointment and my afternoon schedule."

"No problem with us," said Patrick. "We both are runners. Find it keeps off the pounds and helps keep us sharp. I am sure you find it helps with your busy schedule."

"It also sets a good example for both our faculty and students," said McCray. "We are advocates of preventive medicine and healthy life styles in our medical program. So Dr. Morrow and I believe it important to walk the talk, as the leadership gurus preach. Before we start, can I get you anything to drink?"

"No, but thank you for offering," said Nola. "We had coffee a short time ago. Dr. McCray, I mentioned on the phone that we work for the Preliminary Inquiries Branch at the Department of Homeland Security." Both Nola and Patrick passed over their official DHS credentials for inspection by McCray.

She looked at them and said, "If the name Preliminary Inquiries means what I think it does, you check things out before coming to a conclusion?"

"You are correct," said Patrick. "We get a lot of ambiguous information, some of which we may file away, and we also get vague but seemingly credible information, which, if true, could lead to serious security problems."

"So, I take it that you are here today about some vague but credible information?" said McCray.

"Yes," said Nola. "Dr. McCray, before we get to the specifics, I need you to sign a document for us. The information we want to share is highly classified, and we would need you to sign a statement that you understand the seriousness of the matter and agree to maintain the confidence of the information we disclose to you."

"Hmn," said Dr. McCray. "By the way, please call me Nancy. I've watched these scenes on TV programs before but never thought I would be involved with this cloak and dagger stuff." She gazed off towards the window and seemed to ponder a decision. Both Nola and Patrick said nothing and allowed the silence in the room to pass by. After several minutes she said, "Can I ask a question?"

"Sure," said Nola.

"What if I sign this paper, you tell me the information, and I don't want anything to do with your issue, what happens to me?"

"If you don't want to assist us, we ask you to forget our conversation, don't tell anyone about it, and we just go away," said Patrick.

"Well, that seems to be easy enough," she said. She grew quiet again and continued to look out the window. This was interesting, different, she thought. I deal with medical students all day, but here I have a chance for intrigue. What do I have to lose? "I have another question?"

"Okay, ask all the questions you need to make a decision," said Nola.

She smiled and said, "Are you going to ask me to do something dangerous?"

"No, it is really asking you to allow us to do something that has no danger, doesn't involve your students or the medical school, and will occur off the campus," said Nola.

"Gee, here I thought this was my chance to have some 007 adventure and travel to an exotic place." She smiled again and said, "Okay, I like adventure, so I agree. Please let me read your document."

Dr. McCray must be a speed-reader, thought Patrick. She scanned down through the paragraphs, asked for a pen, and signed and dated the paper. "Alright, I have signed, so please tell me your vague but credible information."

"Our inquiry is about your neighbor, Dr. Akil Hakimi," said Nola. "Do you know him?"

"I know who he is; we pass pleasantries when we both are outside our houses, but I can't say that I know him."

"Do you know anything about his activities?" asked Patrick.

"I know he came here as an exchange professor for two years in the history department. He is a Middle-East scholar and has no family with him."

"Do you see a lot of visitors at his house?" asked Nola.

"No. He is renting a house that belongs to a couple that left town for other jobs. They couldn't sell it, so it became a rental. Dr. Hakimi told me he had planned to bring his family here, but, after he arrived and rented this house, his wife changed her mind. Apparently, his children are in what is similar to our high school, and his wife didn't wanted to disrupt their education."

She thought some more and said, "I don't think he entertains or has many visitors. I could be wrong, but I haven't seen lots of people there. I have seen him down on the walking mall several times reading his foreign paper and drinking coffee. So is the good Dr. Hakimi a spy or a terrorist?"

"We are not sure," said Nola. "That's why we're here. We have been given information by a reliable government source that he belongs to a radical branch of the Muslim Brotherhood. The source believes he is here to help with some action against the US or the Egyptian Embassy, but they have no specific information. So it is our job to determine his activities and see if he really is a threat while here in the US."

"And what is it that you want me to do?" said Dr. McCray.

"We want to mount a miniature video camera in your house, directed at Dr. Hakimi's residence," said Patrick. "The camera would automatically record movement across the street and send the photo signal to a remote site here in Burlington. It would allow us to identify people coming to his residence."

"What do you do about the delivery people or people just passing by his house?"

"That's easy," said Patrick. "We delete all those people. A technician can review the signal in real time, and, every 24 hours, the un-needed images are deleted. This camera will also allow us to see when Hakimi is leaving, because we can't set up a surveillance on your street."

She sat quietly and gazed out the window again. After a minute or so, she turned to Nola. "I have a few more questions. What if he notices the camera? How would I explain it, and what kind of liability do I have if this were to become public?"

"Good questions," said Nola. "We have a very professional technician who would come to your house when Dr. Hakimi is teaching class. We know his schedule. The van that comes to your house would have signage of a Vermont regional business, probably a computer firm or a satellite company. The camera would be mounted in one of your rooms on the 2nd floor facing the Hakimi residence. No one would be able to detect it from the outside, because the lens is approximately the size of a pinhole. If you want the camera hidden from any guests using that room, we can camouflage that, too."

"So if any neighbor inquired about the van I would say I was considering having a new LED TV system with wrap-around sound, and all the other bells and whistles?"

"Yes, that would work," said Patrick. "Your name would not appear in any of our reports, and you would be coded as a confidential source. We anticipate using the information from the camera to conduct investigative leads and not for any court purposes."

"And I would have no fear of being sued if I agree to allow you to use my house?"

"We have no intention of making the surveillance activity public," said Nola. "Neither Dr. Hakimi nor anyone else should know we were using your house for surveillance."

"The surveillance is directed to a public street where people can not expect privacy," said Patrick. " Of course, any of us can be sued for whatever, today. Worst case, if anyone threatens liability, you would be represented by the government."

Dr. McCray raised her eyebrows, smiled, and said, "What is that old line--I'm here from the government and want to help you! I remember reading that the Obama administration wanted to punish the CIA employees who interrogated terrorists, even though they had been told it was okay to do their job."

"Yes, things like that can happen in this crazy world," said Patrick, "but I don't think your assistance is in that league. We wouldn't have come to you if we didn't need to have a set of eyes on Dr. Hakimi's residence."

"Okay, but how long will this activity go on, and how will it end?"

"At this point, we are not sure," said Nola. "We plan to observe Dr. Hakimi for a period of time to establish his activities. If we don't see anything to confirm the source's information, we will shut our investigation and go away."

"You won't interview him?"

"Not for this purpose," said Nola. "We might interview him as we do with a sampling of foreigners here on long term visas, but the interview is friendly, and there would be no mention of the allegation unless he said something to arouse suspicion."

"And if he were a trained terrorist, he wouldn't say anything suspicious in that type of setting," said Patrick. "The purpose of the interview is to see if the person is having any problems while living here. A second but unstated purpose is to let the foreigner know that we are aware he or she is here, in case anyone thought about doing something illegal while they are here."

"When do you want to install this camera?"

"We would like to do it Monday, if that would be convenient," said Patrick. "The installation will be done professionally so that no one will know a camera is in your home. It won't happen, but I do have to mention that if there is any physical damage we will pay to have it fixed/replaced, whatever."

"So, if one of my antique vases is broken by your technician, you guys will reimburse me?"

"Definitely," said Nola with a serious look on her face.

"Just kidding. I have to confess, my furnishings are very modern, and I don't think there is one antique in the house. Tuesday morning would be better for me, since I can be working at home when your guy arrives."

"That's fine with us," said Patrick. "Our Technical Services Director is John Carver, and he will be doing the installation. His identification will actually be a photo ID from The Berwick Group, because he is a contract employee of Homeland Security. In fact, both Nola and I are the owners of The Berwick Group but also work for DHS as contract employees. DHS hires us for special projects, because it saves the taxpayers money. When there are no special project jobs, we go back to our commercial clients."

"That is very interesting. I didn't know the government did that for security matters, but then your kind of work is so remote from my life. It really is shocking that we could have a potential bad guy here in this tranquil part of Vermont."

"Well, let's not make any judgments until we gather more information," said Patrick. "He may just be a college professor whose identity has been mistaken by our source."

"By the way, did either of you know I once worked with the FBI?"

"No way," said Nola. "I am retired from the Bureau, but I had no clue about that."

"Well, this was a long time ago, when I had completed medical school and was doing my residency at Beth Israel in Boston. I met this good-looking guy at a party given by one of my medical buddies from Harvard. He said he was from the Ukraine and was doing medical research on the effects of space on astronauts."

"Was he really a medical doctor?" asked Nola.

"Oh, he was a doctor alright, but I'm not sure he ever did any real medical research. We dated a few times, but it was more he pursuing me, because I was busy in my residency. He said his name was Vladimir, and I forget his last name. Then, suddenly, one day I was at the front door of my apartment house, and these two guys appear flashing FBI credentials and wanting to speak with me. After asking me a lot of questions, they told me they thought Vlad was a Russian spy and wanted me to continue our relationship so they could determine what he was up to."

"Lucky you," said Patrick.

"You're not kidding," said Dr. McCray. "I told them I had time for a few dates but not for any real relationship. My residency was my future, and I wasn't interested in any guy from Eastern Europe. My dad is a retired Army colonel, and we spent time in Germany during the Cold War. He would have flipped his lid if I brought home some guy from the old Soviet Union, even though were all supposed to be friends now. Every time Dad sees Putin on TV, he usually ends up calling him a KGB thug."

"Besides dating, what did they want you to do?" asked Nola.

"The FBI guys thought he wanted access to specific medical research at Harvard or MIT and that he would cultivate a relationship with me that would lead to my getting material for him."

"That could have been exciting," said Nola.

"Yes, if I didn't have a residency to complete. Fortunately, the FBI actually caught Vlad trying to recruit someone at MIT's Lincoln Laboratory. Our Vlad was a busy boy, and the FBI sent him packing back to Russia. He really wasn't from the Ukraine, and the FBI guys said he was probably KGB or whatever they call it now."

Looking at his watch, Patrick said, "We really enjoy talking with you, but, if we don't get out of here, you won't get your run in before your afternoon schedule. We really appreciate you helping us. You can reach us at any time by calling the phone number on our business card. If there are any questions, just call us and we will get back to you. John will call you Tuesday morning before he arrives at your house."

Nola said, "By the way, Nancy, if you want to update your TV or any computer equipment, John Carver will be glad to help you. He can get you items at wholesale prices and install them for you at no charge. It is the least we can do in exchange for you helping us."

"Thanks, I'll think that over and speak with John when he comes Tuesday." They arranged the time for him to show up and said their good-byes as Dr. McCray led them to the door. They promised to stay in touch, and Nola said she would call her after John finished his installation on Tuesday in case she had any more questions or concerns. Patrick also offered to let her come by and see the actual video from the camera directed to Dr. Hakimi's residence. He wanted her to be comfortable with what they were recording from her home.

Leaving the building and walking down the hill towards the car Patrick said, "Sharp lady. We couldn't have asked for a better response."

"She was a military brat," said Nola. "She has a better understanding of what we face than a lot of professors on this campus-especially since most of them never served in the military."

CHAPTER EIGHTEEN

Nasheed did indeed have a long grocery list, and they concluded that some items would have to be purchased at a specialty shop in Portland. Destiny had looked in the telephone book that morning and discovered a shop near the Old Port that carried foodstuffs from the Middle East; but that would have to be another trip to town. They loaded the groceries and drove over to the bookshop.

Aarif was standing outside the bookstore talking with a young black man. "That must be Ghanem," said Ben.

Ghanem looked to be almost 6 feet tall, in his early 20's, good looking, and casual but conservatively dressed. He was clean-shaven with a neat haircut and no metal jewelry clipped on his face or ears. Destiny didn't see any jewelry or rings except a wristwatch. He won't attract any attention from the locals, she thought. Aarif appeared to be giving him instructions of some sort, since he was doing all the talking. Aarif looked up and called for Ben to get out of the car and join them.

"Ghanem, this is Ben, my deputy of the operation. He will be in charge when I am not around." Both men shook hands and exchanged salutations. " Ben, tell Destiny the women will drive in the car by themselves back to the farm, and you will come with Ghanem and me. That way we can discuss the operation without them around."

Ben went over to the car and relayed Aarif's instructions. "In case we get separated, are you sure you know the way back?" asked Destiny.

"Yes, I have been paying attention where we have travelled and feel comfortable. In any case, I have a cell phone to call you."

"When are Nasheed and I going to be introduced to our new man?"

"Let's wait until we get to the farm. That way, we won't be attracting any attention."

"Alright, Ben, but you fill this new guy in on the rules around here. I want all these guys to understand my role in this operation, and I am not confident that Josef will tell them the right information."

"Don't worry, Destiny, I'll make it clear to everyone. You just need to understand that Josef is not used to being around American women. He is trying real hard to be sensitive to your status." He reached his head in and gave Destiny a kiss.

"Drive carefully," she said, as he left to join the two men.

"Ben, you drive the car while I continue to speak with Ghanem," said Aarif. "That way, he can concentrate on what I am telling him and not worry about driving." All three men got into Ghanem's car, and Ben waited until Destiny pulled out of the parking space and he followed behind her car.

As they drove out onto the main road, Destiny thought this might be a good time to speak with Nasheed, without Aarif around. She wasn't sure what the woman knew about the operation or what her duties would be at the farm. She also seemed to be more culturally aware about the United States than Josef. "Nasheed, have you known Josef long?"

"Maybe three or four years. I used to volunteer at the mosque, and now have a full time job there. Josef is always around helping our people and giving financial advice. So that is how we know each other. He called and asked if I could help him for a few weeks. He has helped my husband with business, so I felt it proper to help him out."

"I forgot to ask him when I met him if he is married," said Destiny.

"No, he is not married." Nasheed giggled, "I never see him with a woman, and, unless he is giving orders or instructions, he doesn't seem to talk with women. I think he came here to the US after he finished his university studies in Egypt. He is an expert in finance but is also a religious Imam, but a very conservative Imam. Josef helps out sometimes with religious services at the mosque. He once told my husband that American females were too aggressive for him." She was quiet for a minute or so, perhaps considering what she could say about him. She looked over at Destiny and said, "Please don't repeat what I just said. I shouldn't be saying such things about an Imam."

"Don't worry Nasheed. It's just us two gals having a personal chat about men. I never met a man like Josef, so I just wanted to get to know more about him. I won't say a word of our conversation, even to Ben."

"Good," said Nasheed. "Destiny, could you tell me how many people we are going to be at the farm? Josef didn't tell me much, except that I am to be the housekeeper for people involved in a very secret operation."

"Well, it is critical that we keep it secret that more than just Ben and I are here at the farm. That is very important. As far as I know, Josef expects four or five more people to arrive, but I don't know the schedule. I think Ben and I are going to be busy meeting people and bringing them to the farm. We also have all the shopping to do here in Portland, because we would arouse suspicion if I shopped at our local store."

"It sounds that I may not get away to see the countryside. I can take care of a large group with cleaning and meals, but I would like to see some of this area."

"Don't worry, Nasheed. I'll get you out for some sightseeing trips, but we just have to be careful that others don't see us coming or going to the farm."

Upon arrival at the farm, Destiny showed Nasheed to the unoccupied bedroom in the main house. "I know most of your work will be in the guest house, but this arrangement will give you some privacy," said Destiny. "I'll show you around after you have had a chance to unpack. I need to go out and make sure Ben hides Ghanem's car in the barn and show Ghanem where he is going to stay. I hear a car arriving, so it must be them.

"This is a lovely room, Destiny. I will be most comfortable here. Do you want me to also unload all the groceries after I unpack?"

"No. I'll tell Ben and Josef to bring them inside here. Most will go in the guesthouse, but we will be just using the main house for eating until Josef's men arrive; so we will need some of the groceries here. We can eat those frozen dinners we bought this evening, and then you can begin cooking tomorrow."

Destiny went outside and greeted Ben as he and the others got out of the car. "You must be Ghanem," she said. "My name is Destiny, and welcome to my farm."

"Pleased to meet you, Destiny," he said. "Ben told me about you and your farm here as we drove from town. I've never been on a farm before: just a city boy. Your place sure looks nice, and Ben told me I have a big barn all to myself to do my work."

"You can wander around and enjoy my property. This is not a working farm anymore, so we don't have any animals and such here, but we do have these fields for walking, and a stream and pond on the property. It will help pass the time since only Ben and I can be seen in the local town."

"Yes. Josef explained all that to me on the way out here. It shouldn't be that difficult, since I hope we are only here a short time."

"Ben, if you and Josef could take all the groceries into the house, I'll show Ghanem to the guest house. Being the first one here, you are going to have the master bedroom that looks out on the meadows in the back of the house. A very pretty view." He grabbed his suitcase out of the trunk, and they walked off together.

"Come on, Josef," said Ben. "Let's get the groceries in before some of the cold food begins to spoil."

Aarif looked at Ben but didn't say anything. This was not work for an Imam, but he refrained from making a scene. He also observed that Ghanem acted differently around Destiny. There was none of the city "jive talk" when he spoke with her. He seemed more reserved in his manner and appeared comfortable around her. Perhaps there was more to Ghanem than they were aware; hopefully, it wouldn't be a problem. He had enough difficulty putting up with Destiny and her attitude, and he wanted Ghanem to just follow his orders and not question him. He picked up a couple of bags and followed Ben into the main house. He thought that Destiny probably told Nasheed to go rest somewhere just so he would have to help Ben. I need to find her and get her out here working. If this keeps up, that dammed Destiny will teach Nasheed bad habits. We can't have our women acting like these Americans, who have no respect for their men.

CHAPTER NINETEEN

Patrick and Nola parked the car and walked onto the pedestrian mall, heading for the building that housed the observation post across from Java Joe's. On reaching the 2nd floor, Patrick guided Nola to the room where Bruce Thompson was on duty. He knocked twice, and Bruce opened the locked door.

"Hi Nola and Patrick," he said. "I have the inside post today, while Ken and Albert are outside enjoying this lovely weather. So far, it has been quiet, and our professor has just arrived for his daily coffee and paper."

"I'd like to see him," said Nola. "Is there a good place to stand by this window so I'm not seen?"

"Sure, just stand behind the curtain on the right side of the window and look out and down. He is at the third table in the front, wearing a blue sport jacket and light brown trousers. How did you make out with Dr. McCray? Is she going to help us?"

"We had a very positive conversation with her," said Patrick. "By next Tuesday we should be all set up, both here and at the Professor's house. John Carver is driving up this weekend and will work here on Monday and then at Dr. McCray's house on Tuesday. That will make life easier for you fellows and give you more flexibility."

"I am looking forward to seeing this remote electronic capability. I have read about it, but have never been around an active operation."

"Well, John is a real pro with all the technical equipment we use," said Patrick. "I know what we need and our electronic capabilities, but have no clue how to set up and operate the systems."

After a short time observing Dr. Hakimi, Patrick guided Nola over to a large map of the city that was tacked onto the far wall. He was pointing out several of the streets in the neighborhood where the Professor and Dr. McCray lived in relation to the campus, the pedestrian mall, and major streets exiting Burlington.

"Holy shit," said Bruce. "Sorry for the language Nola, but look, look at this. There is a guy who just sat down with our Subject."

Nola and Patrick slid over to the right side of the window and looked out onto the walking mall. Sure enough, there was a young man sitting with Dr. Hakimi. From their angle of view, they could not see his face, but he looked to be a young man with a full head of dark curly hair, wearing jeans and a light brown windbreaker jacket. "Look, he's passing something to Hakimi," said Bruce.

"It looks to be a small figurine," said Nola. They watched as both men engaged in conversation; however, there was no laughter or visible sign of friendship or comradery one would expect between friends. Dr. Hakimi appeared to be expressionless, or perhaps it was nervousness as he looked at the younger man. "Are you getting this on video?" asked Patrick.

"Yes, I did remember to hit the record button when I saw him. However, we can only see Hakimi's face, since I didn't start the camera until I saw that guy sit down. Ken is sitting at another outdoor café just down and across the way from them, but he can't see them. What shall I tell him?"

"Radio Ken and Al Young and tell them what we are seeing, and ask Ken if he can walk in the vicinity of the table and get a better description of the guy with Hakimi," said Patrick.

As Bruce was alerting his teammates, Nola continued to watch both men at the table. Bruce was wearing headphones and talking to Ken and Al. "Patrick, a waiter just came to the table, and the professor waved him off. So I don't think they plan to stay there very long. Oh, Hakimi is finishing his coffee now, and it looks like they both are going to leave."

"Bruce, did Hakimi walk or drive his car here today?" asked Patrick.

"He did drive today. Earlier, Al told me Hakimi had parked his car down on Pearl Street somewhere near the post office."

"Okay. Ask Al if he is parked where he can get a photo of the two of them walking? I assume Al is somewhere near Hakimi's auto?"

"Yeah. That's our normal MO when Hakimi brings his car. We try to park where we can watch the car, but that's always not possible with all the traffic down here."

"Patrick," said Nola, "they both are walking along the mall towards that old church you showed me earlier."

"Then they are headed towards Pearl Street," said Patrick. "Can either of you see any more of the face of the young man?"

"Nola, doesn't he look dark complected?" said Bruce "He also is a few inches taller than Hakimi and appears to be in his mid to late 20's."

"I agree, Bruce. He looks to be Middle Eastern with his dark complexion, but so do some of the students I saw on campus. Perhaps, he really is a student here."

"Well, we do have him on the video, even though I wasn't able to get a 'head-on' shot of him."

"What about Ken, was he able to get anything on film?"

"No, Patrick, he is telling me that they got up and started walking towards Pearl Street before Ken could get ahead of them. Ken and Al are talking now, and Al thinks he can get a shot when they head down Pearl Street. Al couldn't get a parking space near Hakimi's car, but he is positioned to follow him."

"Well, Bruce, even if this turns out to be just a student, it is a good experience as to what can occur," said Nola. "Patrick, we need to get me to the airport, or I'll be here another evening, and the kids are expecting me home. Tonight is pizza night at the Hunter residence and I'm charged with picking the pizza up on my way home."

"We can't deprive the kids of pizza," said Patrick, "so let's head out now. Bruce, I'll see you fellows back at your place. By then, we will know if this new guy is a houseguest or perhaps a student. Al shouldn't have any trouble following them. If Hakimi drops this guy off anywhere in town, see if he can't follow him so we can ID him later."

"No problem, Patrick. I'll mention that to Al, and we will see you later at the house. Nola, sorry you have to leave, but

I'm sure we will see you again." Bruce walked them to the door, and, as they said their 'good-byes' Nola gave Bruce a big hug.

"I'll be back," she said, "so you can buy me a cup of coffee at Java Joe's."

As they drove to the airport, Nola and Patrick discussed Nola's work at DHS headquarters. "I did find an ally there. Her name is Melissa Wallis. She is the night supervisor in their Operations Center. She also has had her battles with Dick Sandelman, the Current Analysis Branch chief. Fortunately, she and I are on 'the same page' when it comes to training analysts. Did you ever meet him, Patrick?

"No, but wasn't he with the Bureau for a long time?"

"Yes, and that is part of the problem. He is from the old school of catching bad guys and thinks reviewing bits and pieces of intelligence traffic to catch terrorists is a waste of resources."

"Well, how did he get his current job?"

"You know how it is in DC. The Bureau had to detail agents to the terrorist operations center at DHS, and Sandelman drew the short straw. He wasn't ready to retire, so he took the job of Branch Chief. Rumor is he really wants Scott Hartley's job, but that's not going to happen. "

"Why is that?"

"Melissa tells me that Sandelman's personality has got him into conflict with others, and Director Wolsey is trying to ease him back to the Bureau - especially since analysis is not his strong suit and Wolsey wants an aggressive leader in that branch. Melissa says that both Wolsey and Hartley strongly believe the Bureau was blindsided by the 9/11 attack because they had no effective analyst function at the headquarters prior to the attack. I agree with them, since I was there, too."

"I'm sure it's my military background, but I've always believed the old motto, 'know your enemy.' We had an outstanding analysis group in AFOSI, and that's why we were successful in both counterintelligence and terrorist operations."

"I know. With Scott Hartley's permission, I have told Melissa about our little operation up here, and she has promised to pass along any intelligence bits that may fit into the puzzle."

They reached the airport, and Patrick went in with Nola until her flight was called. It gave them a chance to discuss some Berwick business opportunities. Working for the Feds is patriotic, but there were bills to be paid and employees needing work. Patrick told Nola he would call her if anything came of the meeting between Dr. Hakimi and the young stranger.

CHAPTER TWENTY

Dinner at the farm came from the frozen section of the supermarket, and Destiny could tell that Aarif was not pleased. She had told him it was decided while at the market that there wasn't time for Nasheed to prepare a proper dinner tonight, and therefore they purchased frozen dinners. She said she would show Nasheed around the kitchen and pantry area tonight and that Nasheed could start cooking tomorrow. Destiny was sure that this plan irked Aarif since he wasn't consulted beforehand, but that was too bad. She also noticed that Ben had not taken any wine with dinner, and wondered if that was because of Aarif being here. Ghanem did join Destiny in having a glass of Malbec with dinner, which seemed to upset Aarif; however, he didn't say anything. She decided to make sure she had wine or a beer with meals, just to get a rise from him.

After dinner Aarif and Ben took Ghanem out to the former cow barn to show him his workspace. It gave Aarif an opportunity to explain the mission and Ghanem's role in preparing the cars and vests for the drivers. He was not told the target cities or where the drivers were coming from or when they would arrive. He was told that the explosives would be delivered the next evening, and he needed to select where in the barn the explosives would be kept. Aarif was worried about someone unexpectedly showing up at the farm and didn't want the explosives to be discovered. The cars would be kept in the barn until the day of departure, and Ghanem was tasked to configure the cars so it was not apparent they contained explosives. He also was warned not to discuss any of this with Destiny, because she was unaware of the real operation. In fact, Aarif didn't want Ghanem around Destiny at all, but knew he couldn't isolate him to the guesthouse area until others had arrived.

Ghanem said he wanted to think over how he would prepare the cars and the vests and would give Aarif his plan tomorrow. He was taken aback by this plan of suicide bombings involving automobiles, but said nothing to either Aarif or Ben. It was obvious this was a big operation and was costing lots of money. If successful, there would be a massive manhunt, and he began to consider the chances of being caught. He had learned as a young boy in the projects that survival was the first priority for him.

There was not any more to discuss tonight, and Aarif told Ghanem and Ben they should all get a good night's rest and review the details again tomorrow.

Ghanem had never spent an evening in such a quiet and desolate place. He was a "City Boy," and used to the sounds and beat of the city scene. He lay in bed and pondered the tasks he was given by Aarif. As he fell asleep, he decided there would have to be some financial preparations because the aftermath of this attack would require him to find a very safe place to hide for a long time.

Breakfast the next morning was quite a change from last night's dinner. Nasheed had obviously arisen early and prepared baked goods to go with the eggs, and grits she served to the group. Destiny was surprised and pleased to be served an "all American" meal, since she didn't know what Aarif normally ate for breakfast. She praised Nasheed's cooking and especially the hot biscuits with honey and butter. She noticed Aarif said nothing but wore his usual scowl when he was around women.

Since there were no planned trips to town, Destiny announced she was spending the day in the gazebo by the pond reading a Grisham novel and working on her tan. Ben told her he had work to do with Aarif and Ghanem and would join her later. He didn't explain what they were going to do, and she didn't bother to ask. She thought if the others who showed up here were like Aarif, it was going to be a struggle these next couple weeks. It did occur to her that Ben's actions and attitude would give her a good insight to living with him, especially with these Muslim men and their attitude towards women.

Aarif took Ben and Ghanem out to the cow barn, and they found three stools to sit on while Aarif talked through the plan again. When he had finished, he asked Ghanem if he had decided how he was going to rig the cars and vests.

"I have a plan that we used in the training camp that should work here," said Ghanem. "The cars will be rigged to explode based upon the timing of the blast from the suicide vests worn by the drivers. I will fix the vest to explode followed by a 3–to-5-minute delay for the car to explode. The driver would exit the vehicle, walk away from the car, and explode the vest. The idea is to draw people to the suicide bomber and then have the car explode to cause major casualties."

"That sounds awful complicated," said Ben. "Are you sure you can do it? The success of this whole operation depends on the car explosion, and we have lots of money tied up in this operation."

"No problem. I did this exact sequence in a practice exercise at the training camp."

"Wonderful, wonderful," said Aarif. "I can visualize now the crowd around the bomber, and then the car exploding and all the damage. It will be spectacular. The brothers will rejoice, and Allah will be pleased." He sat there on the stool mesmerized by his vision of the attack.

"This may also be the right time to bring up the risk of this operation," said Ghanem.

"What risk?" said Aarif, rising from the stool and waving his hands. "We have spent months planning this attack. Our security is excellent: we have used what you Americans call, "Need to Know;" we are out here in the country, and no one knows we are here. When the attack is over, the FBI will be running around the cities looking for the planners and attackers, but they won't find anyone who knows anything about us. The drivers are martyrs, so they cannot be dragged into prison and tortured by the authorities. No, these attacks will succeed, and the Americans will be terrorized, waiting for the next attack." He was so worked up, spittle was coming from his mouth and he was visibly shaking. "Allah will be pleased," he shouted and then, realizing where he was, stopped shouting and sat down on the stool.

"Well, that's all good for you," said Ghanem, "but, when these attacks are over, I will need to be in hiding for a long time."

"Why," said Aarif, "didn't I just explain our security? What can go wrong here? Tell me what danger you see? We have Allah on our side."

"I don't care what planning you do, something can always go wrong. Man, you don't know how the police can mount a manhunt that will round up anyone who may be suspicious, especially if these attacks cause widespread deaths and damage. The politicians will put unbearable pressure on the cops and could even call in the military. No, man, you don't know how bad it can get."

Ben sat there quietly watching this scene and finally said, "Ghanem, we plan to do more of these operations. The FBI will be looking for us in the cities, and we will be in the countryside planning them and preparing the cars like we are going to do now. This is a good plan. We have worked months on it. We plan to bring terror to the countryside so these Americans will experience what all of us have in our native countries."

"Man, you both are naive. Yeah, Americans look soft because of what has happened the past few years. But these attacks are going to piss them off, and, once they get mad, all hell is going to break loose looking for us."

"Are you saying you won't help us?" asked Aarif.

"No, I'm your man, that's not the issue. Whitey hasn't been good to me, either. What I'm saying is, once these attacks go off, I'm going to ground for a while. You guys can do what you want, but I don't want to hang for these attacks. So what I'm really saying is I need money to live until the heat dies down."

"How much money?" asked Aarif.

"Oh, about five hundred Gs ought to keep me until I can work again."

"Are you crazy?" said Ben. "We don't have that kind of money. I thought you were a brother and a follower of Allah."

"I'm a brother all right, but a brother who wants to live after this job, and I need money to do that. It will be years before we can safely repeat these attacks, unless you two guys plan to be martyrs, too. This organization has piles of money. Those Arab sheiks send it over here by the planeload. They will pay this kind of money to cause this kind of damage. "

119

"I can't authorize that kind of money," said Aarif. "Are you telling us you won't do the explosive work unless we pay you five hundred thousand dollars?"

"I am telling you I will do the work, but I need five hundred thousand dollars to live once these attacks occur. I just can't go out and advertise myself as Ghanem the Bomb-Maker and earn a living. Plus, I will need to hide someplace safe, and that costs money."

"That's crazy talk," said Ben. "None of us are getting that kind of money. We are soldiers for Allah."

"Well, we can be soldiers, but I want to be a well-paid soldier. You don't see those rich sheiks over here doing this stuff, do you?"

Aarif saw that this conversation wasn't going anywhere and tried to placate Ghanem. "Look, I will talk with our leaders and see what they can do. But, in the meantime, we have a job to do, and the explosives are coming tonight."

"I'll help you hide the explosives, but you get on the phone or computer or whatever you need to do, but tell your leaders I ain't doing any explosive work until I have 500Gs in my bank account so I can hide out after this is over."

"Putting that kind of money in your bank account will automatically alert the authorities," said Ben. "You know they track all large banking transactions."

"Oh, no. I have several offshore banking accounts, and the money can be sent there. That was one good thing I learned in prison. I took a class in finance, and the teacher taught us all kind of good things when the guards weren't there. The teacher was doing time for mail fraud and swindling banks; he was an expert." He smiled and said, "The warden thought I was just improving my job prospects for when I got out. Tell your leaders that I'll show you how to send the money and split it into the accounts."

I didn't think this guy was that smart, thought Ben. He turned to Aarif, who just seemed to be standing there in a fog. They exchanged puzzled glances. Finally, Ben said, "Aarif, please talk with our leaders today and see what can be done. We need to move forward. It is too late now to change plans."

Aarif sighed and shrugged his shoulders, stood up, and left the barn. "Ghanem, I can see that you really disappointed Aarif. He spoke so highly of you, and now you are holding up our cause. None of us are fighting for money like mercenaries. I'll let you know what he finds out. In the meantime, why don't you set up the barn to hide the explosives and also your work place."

Ghanem said nothing and started looking around the barn. There was nothing more he wanted to say about the money. He was sure they would try some more to compromise with him, but, in the end, they would pay. He watched Ben leave the barn and walk towards the gazebo area where Destiny was relaxing.

CHAPTER TWENTY-ONE

Patrick arrived back at the team house and found all three of the men in the living room, relaxing with a beer and looking at the video that Bruce had shot of Hakimi and the young man. "How did it go, did you get a clean photo of the stranger?"

"I sure did," said Albert. "Caught them coming down Pearl Street and was able to get a shot from the car without them noticing me." He handed the photo to Patrick.

The young man was a few inches taller than Hakimi, had dark features, with black, curly hair, black eyes, and a thin face with a sharp nose that was his most prominent facial feature. He seemed to need a shave but had no beard. "He sure does look Middle Eastern," said Patrick, "but as Nola said there are many students in this town from West African and Middle East countries."

"I got to the corner of Pearl in time to join Al in the car," said Ken. "We followed them, and Hakimi drove straight home. As you know, we couldn't go up the cul-de-sac, but I got out of the car and was able to see up the end of the road from the other side of the street. Hakimi drove into the garage, and, as best we can tell, our stranger is there with him now."

"Well, what's the plan?" asked Patrick.

"That's what we hope you can help us with, Patrick. Bruce and Al never had this situation when they were doing training exercises at FLETC, and I never caught a surveillance with a cul-de-sac when I was with NYPD."

Patrick laughed and said, "If only we had John Carver's camera working tonight. I don't have any bright ideas except set up at the parking area in the strip mall before the cul-de-sac, but that will take lots of manpower, which we don't have."

"Why can't we just take shifts out there and see what happens?" asked Al.

"Because if they start moving in the car, you would need all of us to mount a good surveillance," said Patrick. "So, the four of us would have to be up all night ready to roll. I think the better solution is for us to watch a few hours tonight, get some sleep, and start a surveillance at 0600 hours, rotating cars in and out of the strip mall."

"What if they leave during the night?" said Bruce.

"We lose them," said Patrick. "It's a crap shoot. They could spend the weekend there and never come out. So we have to make some assumptions that, if they leave the house, it will be during so-called normal hours. If not, then we might assume they are trying to hide their travel."

"This stranger could be some friend or former student visiting for the weekend," said Ken.

"Exactly," said Patrick. "We don't yet know who or what we are dealing with, and we need to maintain a low profile. There will always be a time, if necessary, to question Hakimi about this guy. By the way, let's send the photo to DHS headquarters and have them scan it into the system and see if we get a hit. It's a long shot, but it could help us."

"Yeah, that's a good idea," said Ken.

This seemed to make sense to the guys, and so they planned to run a stakeout until 2200 hours tonight, and then resume at 0600 in the morning. Patrick volunteered to take the first watch for two hours so the other three could get dinner. Then he was going to his hotel. They gave him a radio, and he headed out to the strip mall.

There was no movement by Hakimi that evening, and so they gathered at 0600 hours Saturday at Aunt Betty's, a breakfast/lunch place, in the strip mall near the cul-de-sac. From there they could see any car leaving the cul-de-sac. During breakfast, Patrick outlined a plan by which they would rotate their three cars in and out of the strip mall that day. When not in the strip mall, the other two cars would take up positions in the surrounding neighborhoods, frequently changing their positions. The plan would give time for breaks and eating, but keep them ready in case Hakimi departed the area by car. "The idea is to keep moving the surveillance vehicles around so we don't alert any citizens to call the police," said Patrick.

"Should I call the police chief and tell them what we are doing?" asked Ken.

"That might be a good idea," said Patrick. "That way he will know we aren't playing games in his city without his knowledge. It will also give him more comfort about us being here and not playing the role of the 'Big Brother Feds.' Just tell him what we are doing and ask him to keep it to himself, in case someone does call the cops. That way, we can ask any inquisitive police officer to check with the chief."

"This is going to be a long day," said Bruce.

"Yes, and, when you're not on point in the strip mall, you can catch up on your reading or whatever," said Patrick.

"This could be a very boring day if Hakimi and his guest stay home." Upon leaving the restaurant, Patrick made sure each car had city and state maps as well as full gas tanks. They agreed that, unless there was activity, they would end the surveillance tonight at 2200 hours and start again on Sunday morning at 0600 hours.

CHAPTER TWENTY-TWO

Ben settled into a lounge chair in the gazebo next to Destiny and closed his eyes. Destiny was deep into her book, and he could see she wasn't in the mood to be disturbed, which was fine with him. He needed to think. Although he had been raised in this country, he had been surrounded by family in an ethnic neighborhood, attended an Islamic school, and often thought he truly didn't understand the American culture. This episode with Ghanem was disturbing, and he was puzzled. On the one hand, Ghanem said he was with them, but also demanded five hundred thousand dollars to do the job.

It was really too late to find another explosives expert. First of all, they didn't know one, and then it would take time to bring someone into the country without alerting authorities. He also didn't want to admit to their sponsors that Aarif and he had not done a proper job of planning this operation. They did have lots of money and could pay Ghanem's fee. He decided he would recommend to Aarif they pay him his money so they could launch this operation, and then find another expert for future attacks-someone who is a true believer. He disagreed with Ghanem's view that the police would create such a manhunt that they couldn't do other attacks. Their plan was good. They just needed true believers to work with them.

Ben was almost asleep when he heard his name called. Opening his eyes, he saw Aarif peering around the barn, calling his name and motioning for him to join him. Ben thought that Aarif would not approach the gazebo because Destiny was sun bathing here and she would embarrass him in a two-piece bathing suit. He got off the lounger and walked down to where Aarif was standing by the barn.

"Ben, I just got a coded email that our first driver is on his way to Maine."

"Oh, when does he get here?"

"Early this afternoon."

"What! I thought no one was coming until after the explosives got here."

"That was the plan, but I guess the driver was able to get into the country early. You will have to pick him up and bring him here later today."

"Well, I guess we can use him to help unload the explosives."

"Yes. I have the maps with the meeting places. While you were in California, a brother who lives somewhere up here in New England came to this area and selected the locations. For security, there are more than 15 meeting places, and we will pick the ones to use. I have sent a reply that we will be able to meet the driver, and we will use location D today. I chose that site because you should be able to find it and meet the contact without having to take Destiny with you. The less she knows about the plan, the better I feel."

"Yeah, I agree we don't tell her much, but I will tell her that I'm bringing the first driver here today. We don't want to surprise her by just having this guy show up and getting her upset. I also need to tell her that we are getting a delivery tonight after dark."

"You handle it your way, Ben, just so long as she doesn't make a scene when people arrive here. Now, what about

Ghanem? Did you talk with him after I left you both in the barn?"

"Yes. I don't think we have much choice but to pay him something for this job. I agree with you that he really is not a committed brother, but we are too far along to get rid of him for this operation. We will use him now, pay him something, and cut our ties. This will give us time to bring in someone for the next operation. "

"Ben, we have brothers coming here who volunteered to be martyrs for us, and this Ghanem, who claims to be one of us, demands money. It sickens me, and my first instinct was right: we can't trust him."

"Agree, but think of it this way. He does this job for us, and he is never going to tell anyone because he is the guy who rigged the explosives. Plus, I think we should move somewhere else for the next operation, maybe out west."

"You don't think we are safe here, Ben?

"No. I think we're fine for this time, but, for security, we should move around. And I also think you are right about Destiny. She has been a pain in the ass so far. Her attitude is something I have not seen before, and I am beginning to think we should cut our losses with her, too."

"How do you get rid of her?"

"Well, after the operation, I just tell her that living here together seems to show we were not meant for each other, and we should go our separate ways; you know, that boy–girl chemistry just doesn't match. I won't let on my feelings until we are finished here."

"What will we do with her? She could identify all of us."

"Once she sees what happened, she will be too scared to talk with anyone, since she is part of this. She'll want to save her own skin. Also, Aarif, if she gets out of hand we can always arrange an accident."

Aarif smiled, "Ok, but with Ghanem, how much do we give him?

"Why don't you make him an offer of two hundred thousand dollars and see what compromise we can reach. He knows our people are known for their bargaining, and I think he said five hundred thousand knowing you won't pay that much money."

"Okay, I will speak with him while you are gone to town. I also told Nasheed that all of us men will start eating our meals in the guesthouse dining room, and she and Destiny can eat in the main house. I don't want our people around Destiny. She can cause too many problems."

Ben approached Destiny to tell her about the visitors. She had stopped reading and lay on the lounger with her eyes closed. Upon his approach, she opened her eyes and said, "Hi, I meant to tell you I talked with my old friend this morning, Ginny Paine,- oh, her married name is Longley now. We are going there for dinner Wednesday night."

"Well, that is nice, but how did you know I don't have some activity that night?"

"Remember, Ben, we are two people, alone here, studying, etc. Why would we have any commitments?"

"Yeah, I guess you are right. Better we go to her house."

"Damn straight. Her husband, Tom, is a Maine state policeman, so we have to be on our toes. I don't know him, but Ginny's mother says he is a good guy. All we have to do is talk about our studies, and our professions, which are true, so that shouldn't be much of a problem."

"Okay, but we don't want to get into the position where we have to invite them here after having dinner with them."

"I hear you. I'll come up with something. She said Tom works a lot of night shifts because of his low seniority, so I can take Ginny and her baby to lunch a few times, and that should cover us."

He proceeded to tell her about the arrivals this evening, and she didn't seem to be that concerned about it. Her attitude seemed to be, the quicker everyone arrived and did their thing, the faster she could be rid of them. "I really love the quietness and pace here," she said. "It is so different from California. I'll be glad when this thing is finished, so I can enjoy the rest of the summer here."

"So you are going to stay after we are finished?"

"Yes, you do your thing with those guys, and I'll be back in California before classes start."

He asked her for the keys for her Grandmother's car and told her he would be back for dinner. She didn't inquire where he was going but did say she was glad he didn't ask her to come with him, because she was enjoying lounging here in the sun.

He also told her about the men eating in the guesthouse, and she seemed to be delighted. "If you're bringing more men here like Josef, it is best they stay out of my way and eat somewhere else," she said. "Are you going to join them, too?"

"I have to be with them, Destiny, because I'm sure we will be talking business and I have to be in on it."

"No problem, Ben." She smiled and said, "You just won't have any wine or beer with dinner."

"Right. Just save me some in the refrigerator." With that he walked off to prepare for his meet with the first driver.

CHAPTER TWENTY-THREE

While the three DHS agents were having breakfast at Aunt Betty's, Ken's cell phone rang. It was Patrick. When Ken got off the phone, he told the two others that Patrick would catch up with them later. Something had come up, and he had to do some Berwick business before he joined them. "Patrick said he should be able to join us by mid-morning."

Albert said, "I'll bet he got tired of surveillance work yesterday. I'm sure he has done hundreds of them, and this job isn't that complicated."

"He is correct that this work can be boring," said Bruce. "I hope these guys go somewhere today. "

They finished eating and went out into the parking lot. Albert drew the first watch in the parking lot, and Ken and Bruce drove out to nearby neighborhoods, where they could respond and back up Albert. They hadn't been on station 20 minutes when Albert alerted them. "Guys. Hakimi and his visitor just came out of the cul-de-sac driving towards town. I'm two cars back and will stay on him until I can determine where he is going."

"You want us to come in on you?" asked Ken.

"No, why don't you and Bruce hang back until I see where he is going. There's a bit of traffic here, so I'm pretty safe from being spotted." Albert proceeded to tell Bruce and Ken the streets they were taking, so they could follow the surveillance on their maps. After a few miles, he said, "It looks like they are driving to the waterfront. If we stay on this course we will come into Battery Park. Yep, that's where they are heading, and he has slowed down as he entered the park. Looks like he is pointing out attractions or something. Now he is continuing along Lake Street pointing out things as he drives along.

"Maybe Hakimi is just showing him the sights in town," said Bruce.

"Could be. He is taking a left turn onto College Street" They proceeded along with Albert sounding out the streets. They finally climbed the hill toward the UVM campus and took a right onto Prospect Street. "Maybe you guys should close in now, because he could be headed either out of town or into the campus. Now he has his left blinker on to turn onto Main Street"

"Roger that," said Ken. "Bruce and I are actually coming up the hill from town on Main Street so we will meet up with you there. Any sign he has noticed you?"

"No, but when you catch up to me, I'll fall back, and one of you can take the point. It looks now like he could be headed for Route 2 and I-89, since he didn't turn into the campus."

Due to the light traffic, both Ken and Bruce caught up to Albert, who was still a couple of cars behind Hakimi. They continued out of Burlington on Route 2. Ken took the point, and Albert dropped back behind Bruce. At Richmond, Vermont, Hakimi exited onto I-89 heading south.

As they entered onto I-89, Ken told Albert and Bruce he was going to back off from Hakimi because they could follow at a greater distance on the open highway. Fortunately, there were other cars going south on the Interstate giving them cover. Hakimi pretty much stuck to the speed limit.

"Hey, Ken, what are we going to do about Patrick?" asked Bruce.

"Damn, I forgot about him because we were busy following Hakimi. I'll give him a call and tell where we are and we will get back to him later." Ken reached Patrick on his cell phone and explained the morning's activities. They agreed that Patrick would see them when they returned, but, if they had questions as they travelled along with Hakimi, they should call him. They continued south to White River Junction, and crossed over the Connecticut River and I-91 into Lebanon, New Hampshire, staying on I-89 towards Concord, New Hampshire. "If he takes I-93 at Concord, he could be headed to Boston," said Albert.

"I hope not," said Ken. "The traffic there is like New York City. However, I don't know if Hakimi has ever been there, so that may help us keep up with him. Patrick suggested if we get the opportunity we should drop off one of our cars. That way, we would have one car with you two in it in case Hakimi stops and we need to follow someone on foot."

"The only way that will happen is if Hakimi stops at one of the Interstate rest areas," said Albert. "But, so far, he seems to be ignoring them."

"I could use a pit stop," said Bruce. "It's almost two hours since we were cruising around Burlington."

"The Good Fairy has heard your plea," said Ken, "because we are passing the town of Sutton, and it looks like Hakimi is slowing down for the Interstate rest area up ahead."

Fortunately, since it was a Sunday, there were lots of cars and people at the rest stop, and the guys could mingle in without alerting Hakimi. The two of them took their time, and in about 15 minutes they exited the area. Ken had been able to get a couple good photos of Hakimi and his guest with his miniature camera. Bruce left his car in the parking lot and joined Albert as they headed off for who knows where.

As they approached Concord, Hakimi took the turn for North I-93 and then onto I-393 East heading for Route 4 and Portsmouth, New Hampshire. "I wonder where the hell he is going," said Ken. "I would never have guessed we would be going in this direction." There was heavy traffic on Route 4, and that actually helped their surveillance of Hakimi. Periodically, they switched point on following Hakimi's car, but basically stayed several cars back since it was easy to follow him without any compromise of the operation. It did, however, take almost an hour to get to Portsmouth.

"Is there any significant target at Portsmouth?" asked Bruce.

"There is a Navy shipyard there, which is actually across the river in Maine," said Ken. "They work on nuclear submarines. But I don't think they could see anything from the road, and they surely can't drive into the shipyard." As they approached the rotary at Portsmouth, Hakimi took the exit for I-95 North.

As they crossed the Piscataqua River from New Hampshire into Kittery, Maine, Ken called Patrick on his cell phone and explained the route they had taken and that they were now headed North on the Maine Turnpike towards the city of Portland. When he finished the call, he radioed his two partners. "Patrick doesn't have any better idea as to where Hakimi is headed or what he might be doing. His best advice was to just not comprise our operation with this surveillance and see where he goes."

"I have read that Portland is a cool town, but why would he come all the way over here?" said Bruce.

"Who knows," said Albert. "But, if we keep driving north, we are going to have to overnight here. It will be about five hours in the car by the time we reach Portland."

"It's also amazing that Hakimi doesn't seem to be aware of us," said Bruce. "If he really is a terrorist, I would think he would have some training on spotting surveillance."

"It may be he is so intent on following a map or whatever that he is not looking for surveillance. We have no indication he has travelled over here before, and he seems to be careful about the speed limits."

Sure enough, as they reached the Portland area, Hakimi took the exit for I-295 into Portland. Driving along the highway, he took the exit for the Old Port section of town that is also the tourist and waterfront area of Portland. He drove slowly, and it appeared he was looking for specific street signs. Both cars stayed back but did have to be aware of getting caught at intersections with traffic lights.

"Ken, what do you want us to do if he stops and the other guy gets out of the car?" asked Albert.

"I'll stay with Hakimi, and you guys take the other guy. Just keep me in the loop on the radio, so we don't run into each other."

Hakimi drove down Congress Street and worked his way over to Fore Street. He stopped before a games store between Union and Dana Streets, and the visitor got out of the car and went into the store. Hakimi drove off.

"I'll stay with Hakimi," said Ken. "You two take the other target. If he doesn't come out of the store in 10 minutes or so, one of you go in and see what is happening. This is really crazy: drive five hours to go to a toy store! There has to be more to this than we realize. Just be careful."

"Okay Ken, we pulled over before the store, and Bruce will go in and I'll stay here until he comes out. I think we will be okay parking here, as long as I am in the car."

"I'll have to be careful if I have to go into the store. It doesn't look that large," said Bruce.

"Yeah. Maybe you could go in and ask the clerk for help while you look around and see what the target is doing. Tell her your little nephew is having a birthday, and you don't know what to buy him since you're not married and you don't know about kids."

"That might work, and you are right. I don't know beans about kids' games."

They sat for almost 10 minutes, and finally Albert radioed Ken that Bruce was going into the store. Ken came back on the radio and said that Hakimi was heading for I-295 out of town and it didn't look like he was coming back for his passenger.

Bruce opened the door of the shop and stepped inside. It wasn't a big store, and he couldn't see anyone except a clerk behind the counter on the right side of the store. He also saw stairs next to the counter going down to the floor below and assumed his target was down there. "Can I help you?" said the clerk.

"Yes, I need a game or something for my nephew for his birthday. I don't know much about kids, you know, I'm not married."

"How old is the child?"

"Ah four, yeah, four, but he is bright for his age."

"Do you want an educational present or a fun present?"

"Probably a fun thing, you know, kids need something for fun for their birthday."

"Well, with summer coming on, we have lots of great kites for kids. Some of them are really large."

"Okay, let's look at those. Where are they?"

"Just go downstairs. My colleague is down there, and he can help you. When you find something, bring it back up here and I'll be happy to wrap it for you."

"Sure, thanks." Bruce went down the stairs and saw the shelves were packed with lots of interesting toys and models and kites. He looked around, but all he saw was a male clerk who was looking out the window. As the clerk turned, Bruce saw that the window was really part of a door leading out onto the lower street, and no one else was in the shop.

"Can I help you?" said the clerk.

"Yeah, I need a birthday present, but also there was another guy who came in here before me, and we were supposed to meet, but I seem to have lost him."

"Oh, there was a fellow here just a few minutes ago, but he came through down here and went out the door. Didn't even stop to look at our merchandise. "

"Do you know which direction he took?"

"No, the phone rang, and he went out while I was speaking with a caller."

"Thanks, I'll go out here and see if I can catch up with him." Bruce exited the shop into a small alley street and looked in both directions. He could see no one who resembled the target. There were a few people sitting at a small outdoor café, but the target was not there. He turned to the left and went up Dana Street onto Fore Street, and directly to the car. "Al, the target is gone. That shop has a basement level with a door that leads out onto an alleyway. When I got down there, he was gone. I don't even have a clue as to what direction he took."

Albert raised Ken on the radio and passed Bruce's information. "We have started up and are going down Dana Street onto Commercial Street, and will drive to the right."

"Okay, I am on the Franklin Arterial headed towards the waterfront, so, I'll swing onto Commercial and come down towards you guys. Hell, with the crowds here, he could be anywhere, and we would have a tough time finding him."

"Yeah, there are dozens of shops and small streets, and he could be long gone before we could find him," said Bruce. "From what the clerk in the basement of the store said, the target came down the stairs and walked directly to the door and left. So he obviously knew there was a basement level and outer door before he went into the store."

"It seems like this was all pre-arranged and he was meeting someone. If so, he could have been out of the immediate area before you entered the store," said Ken. "I think Hakimi was only the driver, because he headed directly for the Interstate after he dropped the target at the store."

"Well, we know he didn't come back up to Fore Street or I would have seen him," said Albert. "He must have scooted down here to Commercial Street and is either hiding some place here or has left the area. What about we do a couple more slow drives along the waterfront area and then call it a day?"

"I think you're right," said Ken. "We could be just wasting time here. I saw a Denny's restaurant up by the Interstate when I was trailing Hakimi out of here. Let's take one more pass down Commercial, and then you guys follow me to the restaurant. I'll give Patrick a call and tell him of our latest events."

Meeting in the parking lot of Denny's, Ken told them of his call to Patrick. "He doesn't have any good ideas, either, of why these guys were over here today. But he does agree that this was a pre-arranged drop-off or meet of some sort. He is going to ask Hartley if DHS could check this area for any leads or other source intelligence. Patrick says that today's activity does give more credence to the possibility that Hakimi is doing more than teaching here. I asked him to go sit in the strip mall in about four and a half hours to see if Hakimi comes directly back to Burlington. Let's get something to eat and then head back. We will meet with Patrick in the morning."

CHAPTER TWENTY-FOUR

Ben drove into Portland using Destiny's grandmother's car. He worked his way down to the Old Port area and, fortunately, found a parking place on Commercial Street. It was not yet noon, and so the crowds were just starting to cluster into the area. Using a map of the city he found in the car, he worked his way up to Fore Street and found the toy store. He then went down Union Street to the small alley that was called Wharf Street. This alley was at the basement level of the shops on Fore Street. As described in the directions given him by Aarif, there was a small café with outdoor tables and chairs. He sat down and, after a few minutes, ordered a coffee and pastry from the young waitress working the outdoor area of the café. He thought to himself that whoever scouted out this meeting place had done an excellent job, and the directions were concise and correct.

He enjoyed the leisure of the outdoor café scene and was surprised at the number of people, mostly tourists, he suspected, who walked through the alley. He enjoyed people watching, especially the young women in various summer dress. He also kept a watch for his visitor. Almost 30 minutes had gone by, and he expected his visitor to appear soon. In fact, he ordered another coffee but paid his bill so he could quickly leave the café. He worried that his visitor had been caught up in traffic. As he was watching a young woman pass the door of the toy store, he saw a male with dark complexion and wearing a Colorado Rockies baseball cap exit the store. The man looked around and then started walking towards the café. Ben rose and walked up to him. In Arabic, he said, "I like your cap. Do you live in Colorado?"

"No, I just visited there recently to see my sister, and she took me to an American baseball game."

"Are you visiting here to see a relative?"

"No, I am here to please Allah."

The correct words having been passed between them, Ben took the stranger's arm and quickly guided him out to Dana Street, down to Commercial, and to the car. As they were pulling out into traffic, Ben asked him his name.

"I am called Naseef, and I am from Yemen."

"My name is Ben, and my family was originally from Eastern Europe. But we live here now, and I work secretly with the brothers against the Americans. I am one of the planners of this operation and will help you these next days get ready for your glorious journey to Allah."

"I attended University in Pakistan. My family is mostly Salafiist Moslems, but I joined an underground Takfiri group in Islamabad that was mostly students from the University. We talked a lot about killing Infidels but never did anything. So, when I finished college, I volunteered to go to Afghanistan. However, that was not to be. After finishing training in a camp in Waziristan, I was chosen for this operation because I can speak a little English. It is very humbling for me and a great honor for my family that I can serve Allah in this manner. Perhaps, Ben, we could speak a little English, so I can practice saying a few words?"

"Oh sure. I will speak slowly, and, if you don't understand what I am saying, we can clarify it in Arabic."

"I have never been here before or any Western country, so all that I see and experience is new to me. The dress of the women is shocking. No one seems to wear even a Hijab."

"You will just have to ignore all the decadent things you see while you prepare for your glorious day. Our Imam says that we Jihadists must pretend to be part of the American culture if we are to be successful here. Where did you learn your English? You speak well for someone who has never been here before."

"My family has been in the trading business for many generations. My father sent my brother and me to a private school, where they taught English. He said we must have this language if we are to be successful in business. However, my father is a very religious man, and, when he observed the Western countries persecuting our people, he decided my older brother would follow him in business, and I would pursue Jihad, helping our brothers in Afghanistan."

"Well, your family will surely be proud of you when they see what is going to happen here. We must make a video for you this week to send home."

"That would be good. I did make a video before I came here, but have since thought of more things I want to say to my family before I join Allah."

Ben proceeded to tell Naseef about the arrangements at the farm, and that he would be sharing space with people who do not share his Islamic faith nor know the real objective of the operation. He discussed Destiny and her role in helping them, but cautioned that it would be best to keep his distance from her. He also told him that, while Ghanem professed to be a fellow Jihadist, both Aarif and Ben had doubts about his commitment.

"Ben, even in Islamabad and the University we had women who have forgotten their place in life. Their dress is embarrassing and they seem to be caught up in the idea that they are equal to men in all ways. My brother and I have recommended to my father that our two sisters stay home in the village and not attend higher education."

"It is difficult here, Naseef, because of all the distractions, but we will be successful." As they drove closer to the farm, Ben stopped the car and asked Naseef to move to the back seat and lay down so he could not be seen when they drove into the entrance way to the farm.

Ben drove the car up the drive and stopped at the front door of the guesthouse. He ushered Naseef inside and introduced him to Aarif. After the pleasantries, Aarif took him off to his room to discuss the rules for living here until they were ready to go operational. Ben went off to drive the car to the garage.

Aarif was adamant that Naseef stay away from Destiny and the main house and always call him Josef. He told him that other brothers would be joining them soon, but it would take a little time, since they were coming secretly into the country. Therefore, there would be little for him to do while he waited for the others. Aarif told him it was difficult to find appropriate books in the Portland bookstores for him to read, but he had requested the brothers bring some up to Maine when they delivered the automobiles for the operation.

"Will everyone be coming through the border in Vermont? I did not have any trouble, because I had a fake student visa and the professor in Burlington was helpful."

"I don't know. The transportation of the brothers is being arranged outside this country, and I only get a notification when they arrive here. How did you get from the border to Burlington?"

"A brother from the University in Montreal took care of me after I entered Canada. He drove me to Burlington and then told me how to meet up with the professor there. Then he left to go back to Canada."

"What did you tell the Americans at the border?"

"We said we were going to a lecture at the University and would be coming back to Canada over the weekend."

"You can rest here. It is safe, and we will be sharing meals here in the guesthouse. We have a housekeeper here who works for us at the mosque. Her name is Nasheed. She will take care of you and the others. She is trustworthy but does not know what we are doing here. So be careful what you say to her. I'll leave you now and will see you at prayers before our evening meal."

Aarif encountered Ben, who was on his way to see Destiny, after parking the car in the garage. "While you were gone, I checked the web site and found a coded message for us. The driver with the material won't be here until Monday evening, so we have nothing to do tomorrow."

"Did the message tell why he is delayed?"

"No, but I know that he is taking many secondary roads so he won't get caught in those truck inspection places they have on the Interstate."

"Aarif, we could use tomorrow to take Nasheed to town and purchase a quantity of food, because we are going to be very busy meeting the brothers from abroad and also the ones bringing cars up here."

"What about Destiny? Will she go with you?"

"Yes. She and Nasheed get along well, and she knows the city. It also gets her out of your way here."

"Okay, good, you plan the trip with her."

Ben went out to the gazebo and found Destiny still reading her book. She looked up and smiled as he approached.

"This has been the most relaxing afternoon I have spent in a long time," she said. "I could do this for several days just to recharge my batteries. Did you find your passenger?"

"Yes, he is here and settled in the guest house. You won't have to bother with him, because Nasheed will take care of him."

"Good. If he is anything like Josef, I don't want anything to do with him. In fact, I think it is good to keep everyone over there, and then I won't have to put them in their place. Nasheed came by and rested with me here. I do like her, and she is going to take care of my meals while she feeds all of you in the guest house."

Ben ignored her comments and discussed going to Portland with Nasheed on Monday. She agreed and said there were some stores she wanted to show Nasheed, and they could also have lunch down at the Old Port.

"Ben, I'll help you with getting cars and finding these guys who are coming here, but when I have free time I am going to be relaxing here in the gazebo or going to Portland for fun. I don't want to be around these guys, and I don't want them coming into the main house."

"Don't worry, Destiny. Josef will keep them away from you as much as possible. "

"Okay. How about you fetching a couple beers for us, since you can't have a drink when you are eating with your buddies." She flashed her eyes at him and smiled.

"Sure, and I'll bring out some snacks, too. But don't rub it in, Destiny. I've got to work with these guys until we launch them on their way. Then we can have some time to ourselves." With that, Ben headed for the kitchen.

CHAPTER TWENTY-FIVE

On Monday evening, the guys sat with Patrick at the team house and reviewed the previous day's activities. John Carver had arrived earlier and been introduced to everyone. He and Bruce would go down to their room on the walking mall to install equipment after this meeting.

"I emailed the photos off to DHS last evening to see if our target is known to anyone," said Ken. "We have two or three photos that are quite clear of his face. Scott Hartley called this morning and said he has requested the Current Analysis Branch do a detailed agency check of the Portland area, to include local and state law enforcement."

"How about a check with ICE up at the border station here?" said Patrick. "This guy isn't from around here, and I wonder if he came directly from Canada down to Burlington?"

"I'll send Hartley an email on that," said Ken.

"What are we going to do with the professor?" asked Albert.

"He must have come directly back here, because, it was almost five hours after Ken called me that I saw him return down his street for the night," said Patrick. "So far, his role seems to be sheltering and delivering people. Therefore, I recommend we just continue to watch him for a while and see if he gets any more visitors-especially if he takes another person over to the Portland area."

"Then we will know the action is over there," said Bruce.

"Correct. We don't know enough yet to speak with him. If something is being planned for Maine, he may give us the lead to discover it. Legally, he hasn't done anything wrong, and we want to have some hard information when we interview him."

"I like your idea," said Ken. "Now that we have John here, it should make the surveillance easier and give us more flexibility."

"Don't count on anything yet, guys, until you see my work."

"Patrick says you're the best, John, and that's good enough for us," said Ken.

"Why would any terrorist be interested in Maine?" asked Albert. "Bruce and I enjoyed seeing Portland, but it is a tourist place. It seems too small for a terrorist group to target."

"I agree with you, Al," said Patrick. "So far, the terrorists' targets in the USA have been in big cities. But someone may think it is easier to be successful in a smaller locale, where there aren't as many counterterrorist resources."

"Plus, you have the psychological issue," said John. "People expect targeting Washington, DC, or New York City, but hitting a small city could create a perception that terrorists have infiltrated Middle America, even though Portland is an East Coast place. Just think what a bombing by terrorists in Portland would do to their tourist business!"

"Being a port city might make it easier for terrorists to infiltrate," said Patrick. "Cities like Portland are used to seeing people from all over the world. In summer, several cruise ships stop there every week, and a guy from the Middle East wouldn't raise any suspicion."

"Do we say anything to the authorities over in Portland yet?" asked Ken.

"That is a DHS decision," said Patrick. "Personally, I would wait until we had more information, unless the analysts come up with something. Right now, we have nothing that they can work with except to get them excited. You could discuss that with Hartley and see what he says."

"I like your idea, Patrick, and will recommend that to Hartley when I speak with him in the morning. Unless there are more issues to discuss, I think we are finished here for now."

Patrick told them he would stay in town until John finished the installation at Dr. McCray's house tomorrow. Then he was travelling out to California, but would be back in Maine next Friday evening. If Hakimi got another visitor and he headed over to Maine, Patrick would be available to work with them on the surveillance. John Carver would remain with them in Burlington until they could figure out what needed to be done next.

CHAPTER TWENTY-SIX

It had been a pleasant day for Destiny and Ben. They had taken Nasheed to Portland to the Maine Mall for some girl shopping, and then drove over to the Old Port to have lunch at one of the waterfront restaurants. There was a large cruise ship tied up near the Casco Bay ferry terminal, so the area was crowded with tourists. Before leaving Portland, they stopped at a store specializing in Middle East food items and then on to an American supermarket for the rest of the grocery items.

Aarif used the time this morning to prepare to meet with Ghanem and discuss the money he was demanding to do the job. He had come to the conclusion that Ghanem was much smarter than he appeared. He noticed that, when Ghanem interacted with Destiny, he didn't have the slick ghetto attitude and displayed a vocabulary of an educated person. Aarif recalled that Ghanem had mentioned a while back he had completed his high school education in prison and had also taken college courses. Although he wanted to verbally attack Ghanem for his lack of commitment to Islam, he realized this would not work. These Americans were always focused on money, and that was their real god. He would try to use a soft approach with him and hopefully bring down the price Ghanem demanded.

Following lunch, which Nasheed had prepared for them before she left for Portland, Aarif asked Ghanem to meet with him in the library study of the main house. He sat at a desk and had arranged a chair across from him for Ghanem. Aarif wanted to use a formal setting and be seated as they talked. He hoped it would help him control his temper as he talked with Ghanem.

"I have discussed your request for money with my colleagues. They were shocked that a fellow Muslim would want money to carry out Jihad against our enemies," said Aarif.

"Aarif, you have confused me with your suicide bombers. I'm not one of your crazy guys. I agreed to do this work, and I will fulfill my promise. But look at my concern. When these bombs go off, every cop in the country is going to be looking for us."

"No police authority has infiltrated our operation. They won't know who to look for or where we are. Any attribution for the attack will come from outside the country. We will be safe."

"You don't understand, Aarif. I don't care what kind of planning you do, they will come after us. And if you think you can do this again real soon, well, man, you are smoking pot or something. I know how they work, you don't. That's why I need money to live and hide out for a long time."

"We don't have the kind of money you want."

"Don't bullshit me, Aarif. You and your rich backers have all the money in the world. You don't see them over here doing this work. They stay home in their castles or yachts and expect us to carry the fight. So if they want this action, they have to pay."

In response, Aarif looked away towards the window, trying to control his temper and thinking what he could say to him. This guy is a phony Muslim, he thought. Nothing is going to change him. He is not a true believer. I was a fool to have accepted this guy for this operation without interviewing him myself. The brothers in Detroit were naïve. I don't know what he said to convince them that he was a true warrior. He is nothing but a criminal looking for easy money. After a minute or so, he composed himself, turned towards Ghanem, and spoke.

"Alright, Ghanem, we will give you some money to hide, but we don't have the money you demand. The best I can do is one hundred thousand dollars. That should keep you for a long time."

"Don't try that bargain basement stuff on me, Aarif. You got all kinds of money."

"Ghanem, even I have limits on what we can spend for this operation. We had to prepare a budget, and we didn't plan for this kind of expense."

The bargaining went on for another 20 minutes, and finally they agreed on $250,000. Aarif was exhausted from dealing with this guy. Ghanem wanted a down payment, but Aarif would not budge on this point. He was afraid that, if he gave him any money now, he would disappear, and their operation would fold. They agreed that the morning the cars and drivers left the farm, Aarif would have the funds wired to Ghanem's accounts.

Ben had dinner with Aarif and the other members of the team. Several times, Ghanem had to remind Aarif to use English, since he didn't speak Arabic. In fact, Ghanem was concerned that Aarif slipped back into Arabic when he didn't want Ghanem to know what he was saying to the others. Ben observed tension between Aarif and Ghanem and surmised it had to do with the money negotiations that afternoon.

Following dinner, Aarif told the others he would be expecting the driver a little after sunset, and they all would wait here for his arrival. "You will direct the unloading at the barn, Ghanem, because you understand explosives. We will help you, so we can get the driver on the road and out of here as quickly as possible."

Rather than just sit there and stare at each other, Ben turned on the TV to the local PBS station. The program was about people having furniture or jewels examined to see if any were an antique. It bored Ben, but it passed the time without getting Aarif excited about seeing women on TV without the proper dress.

CHAPTER TWENTY-SEVEN

Detective Wally Barnes was running quite late for his swing shift, but Sheriff Tate had OK'd his attending the Domestic Violence Seminar presented today by the FBI in Portsmouth, New Hampshire. Barnes was newly promoted to detective at the Windham County Sheriff's department and had volunteered to attend the seminar, using both his own time and some shift time. The seminar had started late this morning, because the featured speaker coming up from Quantico, Virginia, had a bad plane connection, and so they didn't finish up until 7:00 PM. It had been a long day, but Barnes still had to finish his swing shift. It was getting dark as he came along Route 202, and he decided to check in with the central dispatch center.

"Central Dispatch, may I have your name and location."

"Hi Grace, Wally Barnes here. Hey, I'm running late because the seminar was delayed today, but I want to stop at Paine's Corner to get a sandwich and fill up the gas tank before I come to the station."

"No problem, Wally. Sheriff Tate mentioned you would be late. By the way, congratulations on your promotion to detective. I just got back from vacation and heard the news when I came on duty tonight. When did that happen?"

"Just a week ago. Sheriff Tate told me two months ago that I had been selected, but he couldn't announce it until he found money in his budget."

"Yeah, it's always about money, isn't it? Well, I'm glad you got it. Everyone says you are going to be our sheriff some day, so this is the first step up the ladder. By the way, are you driving your own car now, because I tried to get you on the police radio about an hour ago."

"Yes. I got a new unmarked car that's in the shop for installing police equipment, so the Sheriff told me to take my own car. I just have my cell phone tonight, and you probably don't have that number."

"That's okay. I was trying to call you, because Sheriff Tate stopped by before he left tonight and said you were running late because of the seminar. I was trying to call you to say that there was no rush on getting here. So far, it is quiet tonight, and we have an extra patrol car on duty for the swing shift now because of the summer visitors. Why don't you give me your cell phone number, and I'll put it in the system so we have it here."

Wally gave her his cell phone number and signed off. He had been driving a little slower while talking with Grace and started to pick up his speed. In the distance, he saw a truck slowing down and making a turn into a dirt road he remembered as the Carter family farm. It was a Ryder moving truck. Strange, he thought. Mrs. Carter died some months ago, and the farm hadn't been put up for sale. He speeded up and decided to see who was going into their property.

As Wally turned into the dirt road, he saw the truck coming to a stop up ahead. He drove up behind the truck and saw in the headlights the truck had Montana license plates. I'll bet this guy is lost, he thought. He got out of the car and approached the driver's side of the truck. Taking out his detective shield, he waved it at the driver and motioned for him to lower the window.

Rolling down the window, the driver said, "Is there something wrong, officer?"

"No, I was just wondering if you were lost. This is the Carter farm, and no one is living here right now."

"Yeah, I guess I'm in the wrong place. That's why I stopped the truck. Let me look at the papers again." The driver turned his upper body to the right as to look for something on the other seat. He turned back to Wally, and, instead of having a piece of paper, he had a handgun with a silencer. He fired two shots into the head of the detective, killing him instantly.

Aarif was engrossed in the antique TV show when his cell phone rang. Answering it, he was startled to hear the voice of the driver.

"This is Louis. I'm down here on the dirt road of the farm. Come down here now with a vehicle, and bring someone with you."

"What is the problem? Did you break down?"

"Just do what I say, and do it now. I'll explain when you get here."

Aarif was shocked. People didn't talk that way to him. He was an Imam. Louis had hung up on him. He looked at Ben and said, "We seem to have a little problem. Please get the car and I will meet you outside." Turning to Ghanem and Naseef, he said, "Go over and open the barn. Our driver is arriving. It will take a few minutes, but get everything ready for him."

Aarif went outside to wait for Ben. First Ghanem, and now this driver with the explosives: two nasty people in one day. Aarif couldn't imagine what was the problem. The driver was here. All they had to do was unload the truck. He decided he would chastise him when they met down at the end of the road. Ben came around with the SUV and picked up Aarif.

"Aarif, what is the problem?" said Ben.

"Just drive down to the entrance here and let me do the talking. The explosives driver is here, but he says there is a problem. He wouldn't say what it is. He is just an uncouth individual, and I plan to let him know who is running this operation. I think he is another American Muslim who doesn't know his place."

As they came down the drive, they saw a truck with its parking lights and a man standing out in front of the truck. Ben stopped the car, and the man motioned for him to dim his headlights. Ben switched to parking lights, and he and Aarif got out of the car. Aarif started off by yelling at the driver that he was an Imam and he expected to be treated with respect.

The driver held up his hand and said, "Just a minute. Let me explain. We have a serious problem. A cop came in the drive after me and approached the truck. I had to kill him. Now we have to get rid of the body."

"You did what?" screamed Aarif.

"Please, quiet down, let me explain. If I didn't kill him, he would have upset your operation."

"I am the decider of what happens in this operation, not you. What are we going to do with the body? What about his car? How do you know he didn't call in his location before he stopped you?"

"I checked, and he wasn't driving a police car. It doesn't have a radio or anything. If we get rid of the car and body, we should be okay."

"There is a place about five miles from here which has woods along the main road. There is a dirt road that I believe goes back to some fields and looks to be a good hiding place," said Ben. "Remember, we saw it when we riding around the area the other day?"

"Yes, someplace like that would be good," said Louis. "Here, I have plastic gloves for you guys. Help me stick the body in the trunk, and then take the car down to your place and hide it. Don't touch anything with your bare hands."

At this point, Aarif was more in shock than angry. "Allah, be merciful with us," he murmured. He just stood there as Ben and Louis placed the body in the trunk.

Ben looked at Aarif and his demeanor. He suddenly realized that, although this Imam talked about Jihad all the time, he had never been in the fray. He was a back room guy who sent others out to fight and die. He went over to Aarif and said in a soft voice, "I'll drive the car with the body. You just follow me in the SUV. We will drive down to that place where we saw the abandoned restaurant and the dirt road. You pull into the parking lot behind the restaurant and turn off the lights on the car. I'll drive the other car down the dirt road a mile or so and then run back to you. If anyone comes by and stops, just tell them you are waiting for a friend to show up so you can travel together to Portland." That was the best

Ben could do for a plan on such short notice. He didn't relish driving a car with a dead body, but realized if they didn't get moving they could be in big trouble. "Is that Okay, Aarif? We need to get going."

Aarif just nodded and didn't say anything.

"This is the cop's cell phone," said Louis. "I took out the battery and will get rid of it on my drive to Boston. Just throw the phone away when you ditch the car."

Aarif seemed dazed by the entire situation. He didn't say anything more to Louis. He didn't look at the body. He just went over and climbed into the driver's seat of the SUV and prepared to follow Ben down the road.

Ben told Louis how to drive to the barn, and that two others were waiting for him to unload the truck. Louis told him that, as soon as the truck was unloaded, he would head out for Boston. "I don't know what you guys are going to do with these explosives, but I need to get away from here before someone else sees this truck."

"That is for the best," said Ben. "However, don't leave until we get back. I need to check the road to ensure it's clear before you go out onto it. We don't want anyone seeing this truck leaving the farm." He got into Barnes' car and started off. He was very nervous but realized, unless they got rid of this car and the body, someone would be facing a murder charge.

Fortunately, they got out onto the main road without any other cars around. They drove the speed limit, and, when they got to the abandoned restaurant, he motioned to Aarif to park in the back. Ben drove down the dirt road looking for a place to leave the car. Fortunately, he met no one on the road. However, both sides of the road appeared to be grazing fields for animals, and he wondered how far he would need to drive before he could stop. After a mile or so, he spotted a line of trees that appeared to be a boundary line for one of the fields. There was also a gate leading off the road into the field. He stopped, opened the gate, and drove the car onto the field. He crested a small knoll and got out of the car. On this side of the trees, he could see a pond of water. Probably a place where the animals could get water and rest under the trees, he thought. He could hide the car there, because it couldn't be seen from the road. With the engine running, he pushed the car, and it rolled down the gentle slope into the pond. He didn't stay around for the car to stop in the water and ran out of the field and down the road.

He found Aarif sitting in the SUV, with the lights out and the engine running. He had moved over into the passenger seat, and so Ben got in the driver's side and they drove off. "I think we will be Okay," said Ben. "No one has seen us, and we will not say a word to anyone. This was an unfortunate occurrence, but, if we don't panic, it won't stop our operation."

"You are a true warrior, and I thank you for handling this tonight, Ben. I was so mad I couldn't think. This crazy Louis should have never turned into the farm road when there was a vehicle behind him. He is stupid, and we are lucky. What will we tell the others?"

"I told Louis that, when they finished unloading the truck, he should drive down towards the main road, but not to go out onto it until we come back and give him an all clear signal. We don't want anyone to see the truck leaving the farm."

"But what has he told the others, and what will we say when we return?"

"I also told him to tell the others that we were going to wait down by the highway for him to leave, so no one would see the truck exiting the farm road. That will also account for why we didn't go up to the barn with him."

"Did you tell him not to say anything about the cop?"

"No, but he won't say a thing. After all, he is the killer, and he doesn't want to take the rap for this mess. He just wants to get out of Maine."

"I won't tell our sponsors about this killing, but I do plan to tell Louis' people never to send him to us again. He doesn't understand security, and that will get us killed."

They returned to the farm road and drove in towards the gate to wait for the truck to come down from the barn. After twenty minutes or so, the truck did come down the drive. Ben got out and jumped onto the running board on the driver's side. Louis stopped the truck about 50 feet from the highway, and Ben went out to look for traffic. Seeing none, he waved Louis on to the main highway. Neither person acknowledged each other, and then Louis headed off to Boston.

CHAPTER TWENTY-EIGHT

"Sheriff Tate speaking," said the voice on the other end of the phone.

"Sheriff, this is Grace in dispatch. Sorry to disturb you at home, but I think something has happened to Detective Barnes. I can't reach him."

"Did you speak with him earlier?"

"Yes, and that's the weird part. He called me about an hour ago and said he was in the area and would be in the station after stopping at Paine's for a sandwich and getting fuel for the car. I got busy and didn't realize that almost an hour had gone by. So I called his cell phone and just got his voice mail. I tried two or three more times and got the same thing."

"Did you have one of our cars travel down his route to Paine's?"

"Not yet, but I called Paine's, and the night guy said he knew Wally Barnes, but he hadn't come in tonight. So I thought I better call you first."

"Well, you've done the right thing so far. Maybe, he got sidetracked by something, but...he still should have called in if it were anything official. Have one of the patrol cars ride down that way and report in the results. Then call me back."

"Will do, Sheriff."

"Car 12 here, what's up, Grace?"

"Henry, the sheriff wants you to take a ride down 202 to Paine's Corner and see if you see any sign of Detective Barnes. He was heading down that way over an hour ago. He has his own car, and we can't contact him on his cell phone."

"No problem. I'm about two miles away from there. What am I supposed to be looking for?"

"We don't know. Barnes called in and said he was heading to Paine's for gas and a sandwich, and then he would be in to the station. That was over an hour ago, and the night guy at Paine's says Wally didn't come in tonight. He may have broken down or something. I'm emailing you a description of his car from the DMV."

"Grace, we all know Wally. If he had seen something funny going on, he would have called in to dispatch. He's real good about procedures."

"I know, Henry, and that's what worries me. Of course, with his own car, all he had was his cell phone. Let me know what you find, so I can call Sheriff Tate back."

"10-4 Grace. I'm on my way."

CHAPTER TWENTY-NINE

When Ben came downstairs, Destiny was already eating breakfast and watching the local morning news on TV.

"What time did you come to bed?" she asked. "I didn't hear you at all. What were you doing?"

"Well, we got the supplies last night, and we had to unload them, and then Josef wanted to talk about the operation. So the time just slipped by. What's the weather going to be today?"

"Oh, the weather guy says it will be sunny and warm and no showers today. Did you hear that thunderstorm early this morning? It woke me up with the lightning and heavy rain. I had trouble going back to sleep. Everything outside is soaked until the sun dries it. You just slept through the storm. I don't know how you men do it."

"I have to confess, I had a few drinks before I came to bed, so I was out of it. Any big news here?"

"Yes, a police car or a deputy or someone is missing. I didn't pay much attention. That's probably why there was a helicopter flying over the farm area when I came down this morning."

"Do you think they'll come here looking during the search?"

"That's a good question. Is the gate closed and locked?"

"Yes, I made sure of that before I came to bed. So, anyone coming here will have to call the house."

"Even so, why don't you tell Josef and the boys to stay inside and out of the way. We don't want anyone seen by the cops in the helicopter. I'll get you some coffee while you do that. Nasheed is feeding that crowd now."

Ben crossed over the breezeway and entered the guesthouse. Aarif and the others were eating, but no one was saying much. There was a TV on with the same local news that Destiny was watching. "It appears the police are doing a big search in this area this morning," he said. "We don't have anything to worry about, because the driveway gate is closed and the police will have to announce themselves to get up to the house. However, there is a helicopter flying around the area. So, I recommend everyone stay inside until we know the search is over."

"Do you think the cops will come up here?" asked Ghanem.

"We don't know what they are doing, but, if they come up here, Destiny will go out and speak with them."

"That is good advice," said Aarif. "If we hear them coming up here, everyone has to be quiet and out of the way. No going outside, either, because of the helicopter."

As Ben turned to go back to the main house, Aarif turned up the volume on the TV as a news anchor said, "We have breaking news from our reporter out with the sheriff's search party this morning. Come in, Sharon."

"Ron, I am reporting here from the Sheriff's mobile command post, which is directing the search this morning for the missing detective from the Windham County Sheriff's department. The Detective, Wally Barnes, was last heard from last evening around dusk. A search has been ongoing

all night, despite the severe thunderstorms, and a Maine State Police helicopter team joined the search at first light. The police in the helicopter just reported that the automobile of the missing detective has been spotted in a field about four miles or so from here. Everyone is heading out that way, and I'll give you an update once we get on the scene. Back to you, Ron."

"Thank you, Sharon. We will return you to our regular program, but will provide an update once our channel 8 news team arrives at the location of the missing vehicle."

Ben and Aarif exchanged glances, and Aarif followed Ben out to the breezeway. "Stay calm, Aarif," said Ben. "Those rain storms last night have washed away any trace of our activity. We will just stay quiet here until all this blows over."

"Yes, yes," said Aarif. "But I also went on our web site, and there is a message that two more of our drivers will arrive next week. We can't bring them out here until this entire police activity dies down. What shall I respond?"

"We can say that presently there is much police activity here because of some incident. If this activity is still going on next week, we plan to keep the brothers in a hotel until it quiets down."

"Ben, my brother. You are marvelous at coming up with quick solutions to our emergencies. I would have thought of that idea, but it would have taken me longer to work it out. Of course, a hotel is an answer. Where shall we put them?"

"How about we look at a hotel down in the Old Port section of Portland. The brothers won't stand out in the crowd and can mingle down there until we can bring them out here."

"Good idea, but we also have two guides bringing them up here, and also two vehicles."

"We can keep them all down there, and the guides can keep track of the drivers so they don't get into any trouble. We will find a hotel with parking, so the cars will be out of the way, too."

"Excellent ideas, Ben. After you have breakfast, come back over here, and we can make all the plans."

Ben was finishing his breakfast when the TV reporter announced that the police had found the car. They had roped off the area and would have no further announcements until the State Police portable crime laboratory had arrived and completed the crime scene search. The Sheriff said he had no announcement at this time regarding the whereabouts of Detective Barnes, nor would he comment on any rumors of a body found in the car.

"The area where they found the car is not too far from here," said Destiny. "If in fact there is a body there, you can be sure the cops will be around here asking questions."

"I know. I talked to everyone, and no one will be going outside until we say it is okay." The rest of the day passed quietly, but the 6:00 PM newscast reported the news conference where the Sheriff said that Detective Barnes had been shot and murdered, and that his body was found in the trunk of the car. A full-scale investigation was underway, and the FBI had also joined the case.

On Wednesday morning around 10:30, the phone from the driveway gate rang. It was a deputy sheriff, and he asked to be let onto the property. Destiny pressed the switch to open the gate, and Ben ran to the guesthouse to tell everyone to get out of sight and be quiet. As the police car came up to the house, Destiny stepped out the front door to greet the deputy. A man of about 40 years of age, slim build, and crew cut, wearing a county sheriff's uniform, stepped out of the car.

"I'm sure you're here because of the killing yesterday," she said. "That must have been a shock to everyone. I know we were shocked and saddened when we heard the news."

"Yes, ma'am," said the deputy. "We're not used to this kind of violence here, and everyone is working to find the killer. We are checking all the residences in a five- or six-mile area to see if anyone saw or heard anything. That's why I'm here." He handed her his card.

"Well, the first time we knew anything had happened was when we heard it on the morning TV news."

"When you say "we", ma'am, who is that here?"

"Oh, I'm sorry. I'm Destiny Carter. This is our family farm and was my grandmother's place until she died this spring. My boyfriend and I came out here for a few weeks, looking for a quiet place to study."

"You go to school here in Maine?"

"Oh, no, we go to school in California. I used to spend my summers here. My best friend was Ginny Paine. You know, she married Tom Longley, who is with the Maine State Police."

"Yes ma'am, I know them both. Fine people they are. I slightly knew your grandmother, too, and was a little taken back to find anyone out here. But I see the connection now."

"Well, we have been keeping ourselves hidden away here because we both have some serious studying for the fall semester. In fact, tonight is our first outing. We are going over to the Longley's for dinner. I've not met Tom yet, and Ben, my boyfriend, hasn't met either one. I hope Tom will be able to be home, with all that's going on here."

"Well, I wouldn't know about work schedules. However, have either you or your boyfriend seen any strangers around your property here or heard any strange sounds?"

"No, this has been an adjustment for us, because it is so noisy where we live in California. All we hear are the frogs and crickets at night when we walk outside. In fact, Deputy, you are the first person who has rung the gate to drive up to the house since we arrived."

"You keep the gate closed and locked all the time, do you?"

"Yes. That way, if anyone wants to come up the drive, we would know it."

"Have you been taking walks around your property? You got quite a bit of land here."

"I'm not sure how many acres we have, but we do walk around for exercise."

"And you haven't seen anyone or anything out of place when you walk the property?"

"No, nothing like that. John Hartwell takes care of the property now, and the only thing we have coming up in a few weeks will be a farmer cutting grass for hay."

"Well, if you hear or see anything strange, please give me a call. If I'm not on duty, the dispatcher will send someone out to see you."

"No problem, deputy, if we see anything, I'll give you a call. I sure hope you find the person who killed your detective."

"Well, thank you, Miss Carter, and we will solve this murder." As the deputy got back into his car to leave, she said, "Could you please blow the horn when you get past the gate, so I can close and lock it with the remote switch in the kitchen?"

"No problem, Miss Carter. Enjoy your time here." With that, he drove off down the driveway.

CHAPTER THIRTY

Ben found the dinner with Ginny and Tom Longley to be much easier than he expected. When they arrived at their place, Tom was not yet home. Ginny said he would be along soon, but that he and all the other law enforcement officers were working overtime because of the Barnes murder. They spent some time talking about the case, but agreed to not dwell on it when Tom came home. The women and Ben agreed to make it a pleasant evening for Tom.

Ben found Tom to be easy to talk with, but noticed he was very good at drawing out Ben on his background and activities. Ben was very careful to speak only the truth about these things that Tom could verify, in case he did any background check on him. Fortunately, Tom was interested in Ben's studies with bridges and roads, since aging infrastructure was an issue in Maine.

Tom mentioned he noticed that Ben was driving a car with Florida license plates. Ben responded that one of his uncles lived in Florida but spent his summers in New Jersey at the beach with his parents. When the family heard that Ben and Destiny were coming east for a few weeks, his uncle offered them the car. Being graduate students with little money, Ben appreciated his uncle's offer.

Destiny and Ginny caught up on old friends and activities that were not of interest to either Tom or Ben, since neither was from this area. Around 9:00 PM, Ben gave Destiny a look that indicated it was time to go. It was easy to leave, since Tom had a long day today and it would be worse tomorrow. The women decided they would get together for lunches, so that solved the problem of inviting them to the farm.

As Ginny and Tom were preparing for bed, they discussed the evening, as well as Destiny and Ben. They both seemed to like Ben. He appeared serious but friendly, and Ginny thought he was a good influence on Destiny, who had a tendency to be a bit flakey. Ginny had previously informed Tom about Destiny's family issues and that her grandmother was probably the only stable person in Destiny's life. Tom did relate that, when he arrived home, he saw the car with Florida plates and did a DMV check from his scout car before he came in the house. The strange thing to him was that the car was registered to a mosque in Florida. That's why he had brought up the issue of the car when he was speaking with Ben. He didn't want to push the issue, and figured that perhaps Ben and his family were Muslims. Ginny said she would ask Destiny next time she met with her.

⚜

Meanwhile, in Burlington, Vermont, life went on, with the good professor taking his daily coffee and paper on the walking mall and the DHS agents enjoying the improved surveillance system provided by John Carver. The team believed that, because of last weekend's jaunt to Portland, their surveillance would go on for some time. The question was when would they speak with the professor. Ken Booth was talking daily with his boss, Doug Foreman, chief of the preliminary branch at DHS headquarters. Doug told him that his boss, Scott Hartley, the Operations Chief, would make the interview decision.

"Ken, how are you getting along with Patrick Draper?" said Doug.

"He has been great to work with so far. He knows what to do, but solicits our opinions and then lets us make the decisions. So, I don't anticipate any problems."

"That's good, because Draper is an old friend of Hartley's, and I'm sure he will be involved with the decision to interview the professor."

"Hartley has called me direct a few times," said Ken. "I hope you understand, since I work for you."

"It is not a problem yet, because Scott tells me when he has called you and what you both discussed. He tells me that, once everyone is comfortable with contractors like Draper, he will transfer these people to our branch."

"That should make it easier on all of us, because I don't want to get into any political problems with headquarters."

"Don't worry, I've got a thick skin. Just keep me in the loop, and everything will be fine. "

"Oh, I got an email this morning from Dick Sandelman. He wants me to info him on messages I send to headquarters. I sent a reply that he would have to clear that with you."

"Good. He hasn't spoken to me yet, but I know his nose is out of joint because he wasn't in the loop on the surveillance party you guys had last weekend. When it was briefed at stand-up, he got upset."

"Do we need to report stuff to him?"

"No, but I won't have any problem with him getting information when he asks me. He is the chief of the current analysis branch. His problem is his attitude and big mouth. He forms opinions before he has all the facts. He made the comment early on in front of Hartley and Wolsey that your work up there was a waste of time and resources. Now he has egg on his face. He is also pissed because Nola Hunter has been up in his shop doing training with the new analysts."

"When you have decided, let me know, and I'll copy him on the messages I send to headquarters. By the way, Nola Hunter was up here, and we all liked her."

"Yeah, it's just a personality issue. Sandelman doesn't like her, and he doesn't like outsiders in his branch. I wouldn't be surprised if Wolsey shipped him back to the Bureau sometime soon. Say hello to the guys, and I'll talk with you tomorrow."

CHAPTER THIRTY-ONE

It was Friday afternoon, and the professor had just taken a seat at a table near the outside rail of the enclosure outside of Java Joe's. The coffee shop always put out tables and chairs in the nice weather, since it drew more customers. It was starting to get crowded, too. He had a mid-size cup of coffee, which he sipped as he began reading the paper. It was a sunny but somewhat cool afternoon on the walking mall, but there were plenty of people out enjoying the coming days of summer.

"Dr. Hakimi," a male voice said. There was some apprehension in his voice.

The professor looked up to see a young man standing outside the railing of the enclosure where the professor was sitting. He was dressed in jeans and a polo shirt and sported a full but trimmed beard and a round white hat on his head. There was a bright yellow sports bag on the ground at his side. He had a pronounced nose and sparkling blue eyes. He appeared very much like a person, perhaps a student, from the Middle East.

"Yes, I am he. Are you here for the summer or just visiting for the weekend?"

"No, I am just passing through on my way to visit my aunt. She lives on the water in New Hampshire."

His speech had a pronounced accent, but he had recited the correct response to the professor's question. They were speaking in a low tone so others couldn't hear them. "Come in here and sit with me for a spell. You must be tired from your journey."

The young man came around the railing and entered the enclosure. He sat at the table, and the professor signaled a waiter, who dropped off a menu for the new customer. "I am Nasir Ahmed. I was worried I wouldn't be able to find you here in this crowded place."

"Well, you made it, so don't worry. I saw in a coded message on the web site that someone was coming today or tomorrow, but no name was given."

"I was fortunate to get a bus from Montreal this morning."

"You had no trouble at the border?"

"No. The bus was full, and I have picture card that says I am a student at McGill University. I told the guard I was coming here for the weekend to visit with a friend."

"Did they ask when you would return?"

"Yes, and I told them I would return Sunday evening because I had exams next week."

"Good. Your English is very understandable, so the authorities probably thought you indeed were a student."

Nasir ordered a fried egg sandwich and a cola, and the professor asked for another coffee. "We will go to my house when you finish your food. Tomorrow morning we will leave early for the drive. I have instructions as to where I leave you off and will give you the details as we drive there."

"In Canada, I was told you would have all the instructions for me. It was hard enough just getting here. I was worried about finding you, because no one told me what to do if we did not meet up here."

"Well, that problem is solved, and the brothers know what to do. I drove one of your group last week, and we had no trouble."

Albert Young was sitting at another restaurant, just down and across from Hakimi on the walking mall. He spotted Nasir speaking to the professor and spoke into his hidden hand mike. He liked all these new communication toys that John Carver had brought with him. "Do you see that the professor has company?" he said to Bruce Thompson, who was sitting in the surveillance van with John Carver.

"Yeah, we caught him on the swivel camera located up in the room across from Java Joe's. John also got a good facial shot when he came around the enclosure to sit with the subject."

"Okay, good. I won't try to walk by them to get a photo and possibly spook them. But I will walk them to the car when they leave. Did you spot his car?"

"Yes, John found it on the street behind the walking mall, so we will take him home if that's where they are going."

After twenty minutes or so, Hakimi and Nasir left the table and walked leisurely to the professor's car. John and Bruce followed in the van, and, as they got close to the professor's street, John activated the hidden camera in Dr. McCray's house. They watched the car drive up to the house and into the garage.

"That is one cool camera," said Bruce. "We can sit at home and watch them leave the house."

Ken Booth, who had been listening to the traffic from his agents, said, "I'll bet they don't come out until early Saturday morning and head for their destination. Let's get the cars gassed up for a trip and then get together for dinner here at the house. I'll order in dinner for us, and Al can pick it up when he finishes looking at all the good-looking women down on the walking mall."

With John Carver's technology, Ken could sit at the house and watch the professor's house, using the camera from Dr. McCray's residence. He also sent an email over their secure information network to his boss, Doug Foreman, at DHS headquarters, advising that Hakimi had another guest.

CHAPTER THIRTY-TWO

The DHS team gathered for breakfast at Aunt Betty's. They could see the cul-de-sac from the restaurant, and so weren't worried about missing Hakimi if he drove off with his guest. Since they had no clue when or where the professor would go, they decided to use two cars and the van. While the van gave them a lot of good surveillance capability, it was more easily noticeable than the cars. Albert and Bruce would ride in one car, Ken in another, and John with the van. If they got in a situation where John needed assistance, Bruce would move in to drive the van.

After breakfast, they set up their rotation schedule for the surveillance, and John drew the first shift, parking in the lot outside Aunt Betty's restaurant. They had just set up to work when Hakimi's vehicle came down the cul-de-sac and took a left towards town. The fellow from yesterday, whom the team called the *Guest,* was in the passenger seat. John hung back as he moved out to follow him. He wasn't too worried about the van being compromised in the city, since there were a number of them on the road and the traffic was starting to pick up as they approached the downtown area.

"So far, it looks like the Subject is taking the same route through town as he did last week," said John.

"Do you want me to move in so you can fall back?" asked Ken.

"Not yet. I'm pretty well covered in the city traffic, but move in behind me so I can drop back if we get onto the Interstate."

They followed the Subject through and out of town, and then on to I-89 heading south. As they proceeded south, the team changed positions on the Subject's car at uneven intervals and set in for a long drive. They proceeded into New Hampshire, and Hakimi stopped again at the same rest area in Sutton, New Hampshire.

"This fellow is a creature of habit," said Ken. "If it looks like he is going to Maine again, I'll alert Patrick Draper and have him meet us in Portland, if that's where the Subject is headed."

"That will work," said John. "Patrick knows that city very well in case we need to do some foot surveillance."

Again, everyone was able to use the facilities without alerting the Subject as they set off towards Concord, New Hampshire, where the Subject then proceeded to head towards Portsmouth. Ken called Patrick, who was home in Maine, and brought him up to date on the morning's activities. Patrick agreed to join them, and they set up a communication link so Patrick could keep abreast of the Subject's route and where he could meet the team.

⤚

Ben joined Aarif and the others for breakfast and had plans to spend the day reading and sunning alongside Destiny. However, Aarif had different plans. He had checked the web site early this morning and discovered they had another driver coming in today. Both Aarif and Ben were upset that they were not getting more advanced notification of a driver's arrival.

"Aarif, you must send a message that we need a better lead-time for these pick-ups," said Ben. "Stress the safety issue and tell them we just can't drop everything and drive to the meet location."

"I will do that, but we have no choice for today's meet. I copied off the instructions for you, and you will need to go to an auto parts store and purchase a few things before you meet the driver. The plan is also that we use the SUV that we drove up here from New Jersey. It must be because they know the make and color of the car and the Florida license. There is also a specific time to meet, and so you will have to be careful that you don't miss the pick-up."

Ben read the instructions, which were somewhat complex but doable. "I'll bring him back as soon as I can, because the cops are stopping traffic down the road at dusk, questioning motorists."

"Why are they doing that? Is there a problem we should be concerned with?"

"No, Destiny was talking with her friend Ginny and found out the cops are hoping to find someone who was driving along the road at dusk the night the detective was killed. Perhaps, someone who saw something."

"Are they just doing it at night?"

"Yes, so far, and, as long as we know their schedule, we should be okay."

"But we need to bring cars in here in the next few days so Ghanem can prepare them," said Aarif.

"I think things will settle down by then, but we will have to just be careful. So far, no one knows we are here, and a delay is better than getting compromised. Fortunately,

Destiny gets the local gossip from Ginny, so we should know what is going on here."

⚜

While Patrick was monitoring the ongoing surveillance of Hakimi and his *Guest,* the phone rang. It was his partner, Nola Hunter. "Did you have a profitable trip to California?" she asked.

"Yes, it will help pay the bills for the next month or two. We are going to need a couple more people out there, but the assignment is doable and will be profitable. I'm preparing an email report to you and Amanda so we can get the additional folks out there next week. By the way, I am working this morning."

"Oh, something hot in New England?"

"Yes, the team is on the road and our person of interest is heading my way again with a *Guest."*

"Well, that is the main reason I am calling this morning. You remember my mentioning Melisa Wallis, the night supervisor at the DHS Operations Center?"

"Yes, I do. She's your supporter in training new analysts and dealing with Richard Sandelman."

"Correct. I'm glad you were paying attention, because it saves a lot of time and explanation."

"Nola, I always pay attention to you."

"Right...! Seriously, Melissa gave me a report of a gangland killing of a detective in the local sheriff's office up there near Portland. You probably didn't hear about it because of your trip?"

"You're right, that is news to me. What happened?"

"All the police know is he was heading into work around dusk but never made it. They found him the next morning in the trunk of his car that was partially submerged in a pond out in a field. He was shot twice in the head. Police say it looks like a professional killing."

"Do they have any leads to the killer?"

"No. He was recently promoted to detective; they don't know of any enemies or a motive and are at a loss as to finding the killer. The Bureau is helping, but they don't have any clues, either. I'll send you the report Melissa gave me."

"Ok, but does anyone at DHS think there is a link to our matter?"

"No, not yet. It is just another anomaly. The cops would understand a professional killing in Boston or even Providence, but Portland, Maine!"

"Yes, I agree. We have more than our share of domestic violence crimes and robberies, but a professional type killing is a most unusual crime up here."

"Well, Melissa and her troops are keeping a watch for incidents reported in Maine, in case there becomes any link with what you and the boys are doing up there. I'll send you whatever she reports."

"Okay, thanks, and please thank her for me too. I'll share the report with Ken and the boys when I see them today. If things heat up here, I may not be down to DC next week, so please ask Amanda to send any of my mail and other stuff up here to Maine."

"I may send Amanda up with the mail, too."

"Oh, is our esteemed office manager not happy?"

"She was a little cranky last week. I think she needs a vacation, and of course there has been no one around to praise her for keeping us all organized."

"Well, tell her that Trish and I send our best and have a surprise coming to her next week for all her extra work while we have been gone."

"She'll like that. What are you going to send her?"

"I'll ask Trish to go down to Gilmore's, our favorite fish store, and have them send Amanda a couple nice lobsters. When she was up here last summer, she couldn't get enough of it. Trish took her to Freeport to shop, and, when they stopped for lunch, Amanda had two large lobster rolls."

"Sounds good. I have to go. The kids have swim lessons today, and my Mom can't take them because she is off to a church picnic for senior citizens. Talk to you soon."

After the phone call, Patrick thought about the shooting, but didn't see any link with their case. His concentration was broken, as Ken Booth informed him that Hakimi and the *Guest* had crossed into Maine and stopped at the first Visitor's Center on the Maine Turnpike. They gathered up some tourist brochures about Portland and a map of the state. After 20 minutes or so, they started out again north on the Turnpike.

"I'm leaving my house now," said Patrick. "I'll talk with you when I get out on the road. I should be down in the Portland area in about 45 minutes and will park down in the Old Port area."

"Roger that," said Ken. "I will keep you posted on our progress."

The surveillance moved through the York toll station and continued north on the turnpike. Almost forty minutes later, Hakimi signaled to exit into a turnpike rest stop with restaurants and a gas station. Instead of parking, he drove down and stopped in front of the entrance to the building. The *Guest* jumped out of the car and went inside. Hakimi then drove into the large parking area and stopped. He remained in the car.

"What do you think this is about?" asked Bruce over the radio.

"Maybe the *Guest* had a call of nature. Our Subject did not go inside, so maybe this is just quick pit stop," replied Ken.

After ten minutes or so, John suggested that someone take a look inside, and Albert volunteered to go. "I need a men's room stop, anyway, but don't leave me," said Albert.

Five minutes more went by, and then Albert's muffled voice was heard in the ear buds. "Hey guys, our *Guest* wasn't in the men's room, and I'm walking around the area, and I don't see him here, either."

"He could be in one of the stalls," said Bruce.

"No, there were only a few occupied, and I hung around until those guys came out. I'm just about to start around the building again, but I don't see him. He isn't in any of the fast food lines or sitting out at the tables."

"Could he have gone out the wrong door?" asked John. "Isn't there a set of doors on the other side of the building?"

"Yes, but those doors go out to where the trucks and vans park, and I guess it is closer to the gas station. I'll go out there and see what I can find."

"You think he met someone in there and then they went out the other doors?" asked Ken.

"He didn't come out this side," said John. "Where I am parked, I can see everyone who is coming out into this parking lot. In fact, I have had the covert camera running, capturing everyone who comes out of that building."

"Our Subject doesn't seem upset," said Bruce. "From my vantage point, I can see that he is just sitting in the car, reading something. "

"Well, I'll be dammed if we lost him here in this rest stop," said Ken. "Albert, what do you see out on the other side?"

"I don't see him anywhere," said Albert. "He's not at the gas station, and I don't see him in the parking area. There are a lot of trailer trucks and some big vans out here on this side. He could be in one of them."

"Ken, what do you think we should do?" asked Bruce.

"We can only stay here on Hakimi and see where he goes. If the *Guest* doesn't show up, we have to report we lost him. There isn't much else we can do at this point."

"I agree," said John. "Who would have thought they would make a switch in this place? If he was met inside by someone else and they exited by the other doors, they are long gone from here. Our only lead now is Hakimi."

"John, could you send the *Guest's* photo to Patrick's cell phone?" asked Ken.

"Sure. I can do it now."

"Okay. While you're doing that, I am going to call Patrick, tell him what is going on, and ask him to go down by the toy store in the Old Port and see if the *Guest* shows up there. It's a long shot, but we haven't got any other lead for the *Guest* at this point."

"Good idea. I'm sending the photo now."

᷈

Ben parked the SUV with the Florida plates on the rear side of the Turnpike rest area. He pulled into a parking space close to the building. He was intermingled with the trucks and vans. He had purchased a CB antenna with a suction base and placed it on the center of the roof of the SUV. The antenna also had long pink colored tape attached to the top part, and it fluttered in the breeze. That way, his intended passenger could pick out the SUV and approach it to view the Florida license plates. The instructions had stated that he must be at the rest area no later than 1230 hours. He wondered if all this 'cloak and dagger' stuff was necessary, but had to admit he enjoyed the thrill of doing this work for the Brotherhood. He was able to have a pretty good view of the doors to the building and watched in his mirror for someone coming out and looking around.

Just about five minutes after the meeting time, a slim fellow with a white, round skullcap came out of the building and started looking around. He scanned the parking area and then directed his attention to Ben's SUV. He walked slowly towards the vehicle and looked down at the license plate before approaching the driver sitting in the car. Ben had his window down and looked at the stranger.

"Do you always have a pink tape flying from the roof of your car?" he asked.

"Only when my favorite baseball team is winning," said Ben.

"I don't follow baseball. Soccer is my game. But maybe you could help me."

The agreed parole having been spoken, Ben said, "Hop in the car and I'll start to teach you." As the stranger walked around to the other side of the SUV, Ben got out on his side and pulled the antenna into the back seat of the SUV. Sitting back inside, he said, "My name is Ben."

"And I am Nasir Ahmed," the stranger said.

"Good. Let's get out of here. We can talk on the way."

CHAPTER THIRTY-THREE

On Tuesday afternoon, the DHS team, John Carver, and Patrick gathered at the team house in Burlington. They were on a secure telephone conference line with Scott Hartley and Doug Foreman at DHS Headquarters.

Foreman proceeded to update everyone on DHS checks to identify the two strangers Hakimi had driven to Maine. "ICE reviewed their records at the Canada/US border station on I-89 near Highgate Springs, Vermont, for the dates you saw them meet our Subject in Burlington. Fortunately, ICE was able to match the photos we provided with photos in their data base."

"Was anyone with them?" asked Patrick.

"Yes and no. The first guy had a passport from Yemen with the name of Naseef Al-Shuaibi. He also had a student ID card from McGill University in Montreal. He was a passenger in a car driven by a guy with a surname of Al-Kazaz, who is a lecturer/PhD candidate at McGill. Their purpose of entering the US was to go to a presentation at the University of Vermont. Al-Kazaz crossed back into Canada the next evening at the East Franklin border station."

"Was Al-Kazaz asked about Naseef when he crossed back into Canada?" asked Ken.

"The records don't say anything about that."

"Maybe that's why he chose a different border crossing station to go back to Canada," said Albert. "That route is not the quickest way back to Montreal."

"Could be," said Foreman. "Now, the second guy came into the US on a bus from Montreal. He also claimed to be a student at McGill, and his Nigerian passport listed his name as Nasir Ahmed. He was supposedly going to Burlington to visit a countryman who is studying there."

"I talked with the Royal Canadian Mounted Police Attaché at the Canadian Embassy here yesterday morning," said Scott Hartley. "He was able to do a quick check and found out that neither of these guys are enrolled at McGill. He did verify that Al-Kaziz was a graduate student there. Based on what we reported, the RCMP has started an investigation on Al-Kaziz and the phony ID cards. We agreed to keep each other up to date on our inquiries."

"Does the RCMP know how the two guys in Maine got into Canada?" asked Patrick.

"No. That's going to be one of the issues the RCMP will investigate. Supposedly, both these guys were legally in Canada as students, but now that's open to question. We have good relations with the RCMP Attaché here, so he'll let us know what they find out," said Hartley.

"We'll send you a hard copy of the IDs and physical descriptions of the two guys in Maine," said Foreman.

"Are we going to put out an alert now on the two guys in Maine?" asked Ken. "They are here under false pretenses."

"Not yet," said Hartley. "We need to know some more information before we contact the police in Maine. And that leads into the question of when we interview the professor."

"I think we have enough now to talk with him," said Patrick.

"I agree," said Hartley. "We need to get some insight into what is going on, and the professor is vulnerable, since he can be sent home. However, we need to plan out how we do the interview."

"I have some thoughts on that," said Patrick. "If we do it right, we can avoid a potential pissing match with the people at State, since Hakimi is here under their auspices."

"Who is going to do the interview?" asked Ken.

"Well, I thought you and Patrick should be the interviewers," said Hartley. "What do you think, Patrick?"

"Agree. Ken has experience from his police department days, and we really need a young guy and an older guy to play off the Subject."

"How do you mean?" asked Bruce.

"Hakimi is older than Ken and younger than me," said Patrick. "We may have to play the old good guy-bad guy scenario with him, depending on his reaction to us. We don't know what kind of interrogation training he has been given, if any at all. So we'll work out some possible scenarios before we meet him."

"You play the good guy?" asked Ken.

"That's right," said Patrick. "If he is looking for support in the interview he'll be looking at me...Mr. Softy. You are too young for that role, Ken."

"Well, that's why I get paid the big bucks," said Ken. "I also like being the hardass."

"Okay," said Hartley. "You two guys work up how you're going to do the interview, chat about it with Doug, and let's see if we can be ready to go by Thursday. Is that doable?"

"It's a plan," said Patrick. "We'll talk with you both once we have everything set to go."

When the conference call was concluded, Doug Foreman said to Hartley, "I'm glad Patrick agreed to do the interview with Ken. Albert and Bruce are too inexperienced."

"Yes, and if we sent someone up there from here they wouldn't like it," said Hartley. "Patrick has bonded with our guys, so there won't be any jealousy."

"It also could be good training for our guys, since you know that Patrick will organize and run scenarios with them before they approach Hakimi," said Doug.

"Yes, and, Doug, we need to get some information out of this guy before something happens in Maine."

"I can see the Congressional hearings now," said Doug.

"And how long did you have this terrorist under surveillance, Mr. Hartley, and you didn't do anything!"

"Now, now," said Hartley. "You know our esteemed Congressmen never second guess us investigators."

"Right!"

CHAPTER THIRTY-FOUR

Meanwhile, back in Maine, Aarif and Ben had been busy planning for new arrivals; however, the housing arrangements had been altered. Ben and Nasir Ahmed had no trouble returning to the farm on Sunday. Ben turned Nasir over to Aarif so he could explain all the rules about living here, and Ben sought out Destiny, who was reading outside by the pond. She was not in a good mood. Apparently, Nasheed had mentioned to Destiny that her clothes embarrassed Josef, and he was concerned that this would corrupt the young men arriving at the farm. He had asked Nasheed to say something to Destiny, hoping that she would wear more conservative clothing. Unfortunately, it had the opposite effect. Destiny said nothing to Nasheed, but, when Ben returned, she unloaded on him.

She had been stewing about Josef's comments all afternoon and decided she had had enough of this man. She told Ben that no more of these "creepy" fundamentalists were to stay at the farm. Anyone else arriving could stay in Portland until they were ready to activate the plan. Ben had tried to overcome her objections, but she was adamant. In fact, she told Ben she had considered making everyone leave, but decided it could cause bigger problems and risk her security and reputation in the community. At this point, she just wanted this operation to be over with and everyone, including Ben, to leave, so she could enjoy the rest of the summer here in Maine.

Aarif became quite excited when Ben gave him the news about housing the new arrivals in Portland. "This is not working out how we had planned the operation. This Destiny is creating problems. Maybe we should get rid of her now."

"That won't help us at all," said Ben. "We need her until we are ready to leave here. I thought, because she was naïve, I could control her. But she does have a stubborn streak, and she doesn't like our brothers. I believe we can house the new people in Portland without risking the operation. Let me check out the hotels in Portland tomorrow."

"Okay, Ben, you set up the arrangements, because the rest of our brothers are coming this week. You see now why we Muslims control our women. This Destiny is a harlot who hates our people and religion. We need to get rid of her when we leave."

"I agree with you now, Aarif. But just stay calm until we are ready to leave. You and the others stay away from Destiny, and I'll pretend everything is fine between her and me. We don't want her to get wise to our real goals or so upset that she runs to her friends here. That would be a disaster."

"Yes, she could tell them anything about us, and they would believe her. Ben, play the boyfriend until the end, and then we find a way to silence her."

The next day, Ben drove into Portland and selected the Residence hotel down near the Visitor's Center in the Old Port area. He figured that four foreign-looking men staying in this area of town would attract less attention, since this was a prime tourist spot to include visitors arriving here on cruise ships. A reservation was made using the names Aarif had given him. Ben had a credit card in a cover name provided by Aarif, and that card was used for payment. The men were to arrive on Wednesday in two separate vehicles, since the cars were needed for the attacks on July 4th. The two Jihadists from St. Maarten were to be accompanied by two young men, who were sons of a dear friend of Aarif. The men had legally come into the US as students from Yemen, but had completed their studies. Both men, whom Aarif called Umar and Awad, possessed forged British student identity cards because they had spent time as students in the UK, and spoke good English. Their task was to bring Samir and Rabiah up to Maine from New Jersey, having them drive on US roads so they would become comfortable driving to their ultimate destinations. They would stay with the Jihadists in Portland until the time for the operation, and then fly back to New Jersey from Boston. The cars from New Jersey would be picked up by Ben and the two Jihadists staying at the farm so Ghanem could prepare them for the operation.

Ben realized that he had to take charge of these unexpected changes to their operation. Aarif was good at laying out the overall scenario, but became excited and somewhat unstable when events didn't go as he had planned them. Destiny enjoyed toying with Aarif and knew how to get him so wound up that he had trouble thinking straight. Ben had never seen this side of Destiny and knew he would have to find a way to eliminate her as a threat. He had enjoyed sex with her, but she was now grating on him, too. Whatever he did, it would have to look like an accident. Ben wanted no trace of this operation or Destiny's demise linked to him. He had noticed Ghanem giving Destiny close inspection when he thought Ben was not looking. Perhaps he should talk with him. He could offer Ghanem an opportunity to play with Destiny and take care of her when he was finished. This could work out for both of them.

CHAPTER THIRTY-FIVE

On Thursday afternoon, Ken and Patrick observed the professor arriving at a table outside Java Joe's, where he would sip coffee and read his newspaper. "Let's allow him to settle in and drink some of his coffee, and then we'll approach him," said Patrick. Using the hidden wrist mike, he checked to see if everyone on the team was in place. "I don't expect any trouble, but you never know what a person will do when approached by the cops...especially a foreigner."

After five minutes or so, he said, "Okay, let's go. I'll make the introductions."

They flanked the professor as they came to his table. He looked up, turning his head from Ken to Patrick. "Professor Hakimi, I am Special Agent Draper, and this is Special Agent Booth. We are from the Department of Homeland Security. Can we sit, and we'll show you our credentials?"

"Yes--- but why do you want to talk with me?"

"We will get to that in a minute," said Patrick. They both sat down on either side of the professor and produced their credentials. He gave them a cursory look and then looked up at Patrick.

"I ask again, why do you want to speak to me? I am a visiting professor here at the University. I teach students and have no time for other things." Hakimi seemed to regain his composure as he attempted to assert his position as a professor. His manner of speech took on that attitude, too.

"That's precisely why we want to talk with you, professor," said Patrick. "You may have some insight into a problem we are working on here in Vermont."

"What problem? I teach Middle East history to under-graduates, as well as contemporary problems in a graduate seminar. I know nothing about your security."

"I would be happy to explain this in detail," said Patrick. "We would prefer if you could accompany us to an office down the walking mall at City Hall, where we can speak in private."

"I don't have time for such discussion." His speech was beginning to get a bit haughty. "I have a class to teach and don't have time for your problems."

"Listen, professor," said Ken, "we checked, and you don't have any other classes this afternoon."

Hakimi gave Ken a dirty look. "You have been checking on me?"

"We just wanted to speak with you when you had an afternoon free," said Patrick.

"Professor," said Ken, "we can go down to our office now and have a nice chat, or I can get a Federal judge to issue a warrant and, tomorrow morning when you are in front of your class, two U.S. Marshalls will come into your classroom, serve the warrant, and escort you down to our office."

Hakimi glared at Ken. Obviously, he was not used to this tone or manner of speech. After a few seconds, he turned towards Patrick. "If I must, but I can only spare a short time. I have class preparations to do."

"Thank you, professor," said Patrick. "This shouldn't take too long, and your assistance will greatly help us." They got up from the table and walked down the mall towards the corner of Main Street and the end of the walking mall. The police chief had arranged for them to have two rooms in the basement of the building, where John Carver had installed covert cameras and audio equipment. The furniture in the interview room was basically a table and chairs, a coat rack, and bookcases. A solid door connected the rooms. There was warm track lighting along the ceiling. The rooms were normally used by staff for research purposes, and thus there were a number of bookcases along the walls filled with ledgers and other official-looking books. There were no windows.

The walk to City Hall had been somewhat strained. Patrick tried to engage the professor in a conversation about living here in Vermont and his impression of the American lifestyle as compared to life in Egypt. Hakimi gave perfunctory responses, but offered little insight into his true feelings for America or its people. He did mention that students here were less respectful to faculty than in his own country.

Entering the basement rooms of City Hall, they sat at the large, rectangular table, with Ken and Patrick sitting across from Hakimi. "Now, what is it that is so secret that we have had to come down here to talk?" asked Hakimi.

"Professor, we are looking into a matter of foreign students coming into Vermont from Canada. These are mostly young people from the Middle East who claim to be students at McGill University in Montreal. We were wondering if anyone who fits this profile had tried to contact you," said Patrick.

Francis Dillon

Hakimi looked somewhat puzzled but didn't say anything. Ken and Patrick just sat and waited for him to reply. Patrick wondered if the professor was trying to put together a story that would appear innocent to them. He had rehearsed with Ken the opening question and told him they would just sit and wait for Hakimi to respond, even if it took a while for him to answer. The question would undoubtedly cause Hakimi to wonder if his activities had been compromised, or if this was just an innocent inquiry, since he was from the Middle East and it would be natural for students from the Middle East to contact him.

"I run into foreign students all the time," said Hakimi. "I see them on campus, they approach me when I am sitting in the walking mall or even a restaurant. It is natural, since I look like a foreigner and my students know I am an exchange professor."

"Have you met many foreign students here who say they are studying at McGill University?" asked Ken.

"I can't recall. I meet so many students and other people on the campus and in town. It is possible, but I don't remember anyone."

"How about students who just say they are studying in Canada?" asked Ken.

Hakimi gave him an annoyed look and said, "Young man, I just told you that I meet many people every day, and, while it is possible, I don't remember meeting any Canadian students who are studying at McGill."

"Have you ever visited McGill?" asked Patrick. "It is a very nice campus, right in the heart of Montreal."

"No. I haven't had the chance to do any traveling since my arrival. I hope to do some later this summer, after I return from seeing my family in Egypt."

"It must be hard working here, with your family back home," said Patrick. "I travel a bit, but I enjoy being home. Is there any chance your family could join you in the fall?"

"We had hoped for all my family to be here this year, but it was not possible, because my oldest son wanted to finish school with his classmates. I don't know what we will do when the new term starts this fall. I must talk with my family when I go home."

Patrick noticed that Hakimi had started to relax, and his speech soften a bit when they talked about family. It was time to give him a little jab. He nodded to Ken to take over.

"Professor, have you ever met a foreign student by the name of Nasir Ahmed since you have been here?" asked Ken.

Hakimi look startled and started to speak. However, he caught himself and acted like he was thinking over Ken's question. "That name doesn't seem to be familiar. As I said, I meet so many young people." He spoke softly and didn't seem to be as upset with Ken. However, they noticed his eyes blink when he heard the name, and he squirmed a bit in his chair.

Ken and Patrick just sat without speaking, waiting for the professor to proceed. They thought it interesting that Hakimi didn't ask why they were inquiring about Ahmed, or their interest in foreign students attending McGill. When it was apparent that he was not going to say anything else, Ken threw out the name of Naseef from Yemen and asked if he had ever met him. They noticed a few sweat beads on his forehead at the hairline and the repeated crossing of his fingers. He seemed to compose himself before answering Ken's question.

"I draw a blank on that name, too. As I said, I am unable to assist you. If there isn't any more to discuss, I need to leave. I have preparations for class tomorrow." He started to stand, as if to leave the room.

Patrick nodded to Ken, who said "Professor, if you don't know these gentlemen, why did take them to your home?"

Hakimi whirled around and almost shouted at Ken. "Who I invite to my home is my business, but I don't know those names. Are you following me?"

Ken ignored his question. "Professor, if you invited them to your house, they must have told you something about their travels or where they were studying, if they were students. Anything you can tell us will be helpful."

"Are you calling me a liar?" He sat back down and glared at Ken. It appeared he was trying to bluff and bluster his way out of this conversation.

Ken said, "Professor, I understand you took each of these two fellows on a long drive, so you must have learned something about them?"

It seemed to suddenly dawn on Hakimi that he had stopped denying that he knew the two individuals and that his story was not very coherent. "So what," he shouted, "I am approached by foreign students, and I offer to help them. I can't remember names, and what crime is there in helping people? Tell me!"

As Hakimi's voice level rose, Ken spoke softer to him, almost a whisper. "Professor, since you spent a couple of days with these people, it only stands to reason that you learned something about them. We would like you to share that knowledge."

Hakimi just sat there. Being an intelligent man, he realized he had talked his way into a story that didn't make sense. He was now perspiring, and his hands trembled. Patrick and Ken just sat there and stared at him. Finally, he lowered his head and, in a low voice, said, "Obviously, you have some information about me and these men. But I have nothing more to say."

Hakimi rose, pushed his chair back, and started for the door. His hand was just reaching for the doorknob when Ken said, "What will happen, Professor, when the word gets back to certain circles in Egypt that you have been working with American Intelligence?"

"That is a lie, and you can't do this to me. I shall report you to your superiors. You have rules to follow. Don't try to bluff me." He turned towards Patrick. "Tell him. Tell this crazy man that you have laws and rules to follow. You can't do this to me."

Patrick said, "Professor, we don't have to follow the rules. We are not the police or the FBI, and my partner is correct we - will send that story back to Egypt."

Hakimi took his hand off the doorknob and approached the table. He looked at both men and said, "You are bluffing."

Patrick said, "Walk out that door now, professor, and you will find that we are not bluffing. When it comes to protecting America and our people, we throw out the rulebook.

Remember water boarding? You have a choice: Cooperate, and we will protect you. If not, I can guarantee you will have some interesting visitors when you return home this summer."

Hakimi slowly lowered himself into the chair and bowed his head. His body trembled, and he began to sob. "You do not understand, you do not understand," he said softly, amidst his tears.

CHAPTER THIRTY-SIX

The afternoon Jet Blue flight from St. Maarten landed at Kennedy Airport in New York on schedule. Passenger Rabiah Abdou lived on the Dutch side of the island in Phillipsburg and was employed as a cook. When questioned at Immigration about his purpose in the United States, he said he was a sous-chef at a hotel in St. Maarten and going to a culinary conference at Johnson and Wales University in Providence, Rhode Island. He expected to be in the United States less than a week and listed his US address at the University. His passport issued by the Dutch Netherlands Antilles government seemed to be in order, and he was passed on through US Customs.

Upon leaving the Customs area, Abdou proceeded out into the main terminal and found a quiet spot. Using his cell phone, he dialed a number sent to him earlier in St. Maarten. The person who answered on the other end directed him to go out the front door of the terminal and look for a limo driver with a sign having his surname name on it. The driver would take him to his destination.

Rabiah did as he was told. He saw a number of limos outside the terminal with their drivers holding signs with names on them. He finally saw a male holding a sign with his name on it. He approached and said, "I was told you are the man that will take me to victory."

The driver replied, "I am one of many who will lead you there."

The agreed-on parole being correct, Rabiah smiled and followed the driver to the car. His destination this afternoon was a house in the Oranges section of New Jersey, not far off of the Garden State Parkway.

About an hour after Mr. Abdou landed at JFK, a male by the name of Samir Dahar arrived at Newark International airport on a Continental Airlines flight from St. Maarten. He purported to be a pastry chef living and working on the French side of the Island. He was a French Algerian who allegedly came to St. Maarten from Marseille, France, and possessed a French passport. When questioned at Immigration, he stated his purpose was to attend a culinary conference at Johnson and Wales University in Rhode Island. He also gave his US address at the University and said he planned to be in the US for less than a week.

Upon leaving the US Customs area, Mr. Dahar entered the main terminal area and proceeded to follow the same procedures as Mr. Abdou had done at JFK. Within 10 minutes, he had located his limo driver, and they set off for the Oranges in New Jersey.

Neither Abdou nor Dahar had known each other in St. Maarten. Both were volunteers for Jihad and had been independently sent to the island to await assignment. Each had been told it may be a long time, even years, before they were activated. They each were given a different web site to check weekly, as well as passwords and a coded message that would provide instructions when the time came for action. Both men had actually studied culinary arts in France and were easily able to attain employment in St. Maarten, due to the large number of hotels and restaurants on the island. The turnover in kitchens on the island was large, and so no one paid detailed attention to one's background, as long as they could do the work. The men were told they would be shocked by the dress and actions of tourists coming to the island. They also were not to make attachments to anyone there. However, the atmosphere on the island would provide them good cover for their eventual sacrifice for Allah.

Both men spoke enough English to get by. Their interaction with tourists on St. Maarten prepared them for the way of life they would encounter in mainland US. The biggest adjustment for them was getting used to the traffic they encountered riding to the safe house in New Jersey. They would rest the next day and prepare for the drive to Maine. Both had international driver's licenses and were given a driver's manual to study US traffic signs. Their two hosts, Umar and Awad, who had picked them each up at the airport, told them they would practice driving on the way to Maine, so they would feel comfortable driving alone when it came time for the operation.

Abdou talked excitedly about their coming operation, but Dahar said little and appeared to be just going along with his instructions. It was apparent from his statements that Abdou was a radical who could not wait to sacrifice himself for Allah. While Umar and Awad were Jihadists, they had no desire to leave mother earth so soon; in fact, they enjoyed the pleasures of Western life. They were scheduled to leave the US, but postponed their travel a few weeks so they could help Aarif.

None of the men knew the details of the coming operation, except that the Jihadists had to be able to drive a car and follow traffic directions. Abdou and Dahar were volunteers who would sacrifice their life for Allah. The New Jersey Jihadists were to get the other two men to Portland and stay with them until contacted by Aarif. Once their assignment was complete, they were to fly out of the country to Holland and on to the Middle East. Umar and Awad were brothers and came from a prominent Muslim family in

Yemen. Their father was a long-time friend of Aarif, and they had been sent to the US to study Western-banking practices after attaining university degrees in the UK. They had been radicalized while studying in the UK, but their Jihadists ties were more intellectual rather than operational. No self-sacrifice for them!

CHAPTER THIRTY-SEVEN

Patrick and Ken allowed Professor Hakimi time to compose himself before pursuing his outburst of not understanding. Patrick gave him a glass of water and sat down across from him. After a while, he said, "Professor, we can be understanding of your plight, whatever it is, and help you with whatever problem you have encountered. All you have to do is tell us the facts of your involvement, but you must be truthful with us. Otherwise, we can't help you."

Patrick wasn't in a hurry to rush Hakimi. In fact, while they sat here, John Carver had quietly entered the professor's home. He was to download everything from the Professor's computer and install some kind of monitor that would allow them to remotely trace and read his email. Patrick didn't understand how all this was done electronically, but had complete trust in Carver's ability to do the job without compromise of their interest. Based on Hakimi's activities, they had approval from the secret FISA Court to intercept his telephone calls and the Internet traffic.

Hakimi said nothing for a few minutes. He looked carefully into Patrick's eyes, and Patrick hoped that Hakimi would view him as a person he could trust. Patrick smiled, but said nothing.

"You know a lot about me?" Hakimi asked.

"We know enough about your activities to realize you are involved somehow in a possible terrorist plot," said Patrick.

"I am not a terrorist. I am a professor with an international reputation, who came here to teach your students about my country and its history. Why would I want to be involved with terrorists?"

"Could it be that you are a member of the Muslim Brotherhood?" said Ken.

"Many years ago, at university, I was an active member of the Brotherhood, similar to many of your professors in the 1950s who were members of the Communist Party. It was an intellectual pursuit. We wanted greatness for Egypt again, and the Brotherhood offered that possibility. They also provided needed humanitarian services that the government wouldn't provide. I came from a poor family. The Brotherhood allowed me to complete my university studies."

"When did you leave the Brotherhood?" asked Ken.

"Intellectually, I never really left. On the surface, no one knew of my past activities. Otherwise, I couldn't secure a position at the university. I grew up in Luxor and did my early studies there. I was able to go to England for my doctoral studies. When I returned to Egypt, I lived in Cairo. So no one knew of my past life in Luxor and the UK. I don't and never have supported violence or overthrow of the government. But I do believe in regaining the grandeur of my country."

"Well, how did that lead to your involvement with these two men you drove to Maine?" said Patrick.

"As you know, in the overthrow of the Mubarak government, the Brotherhood was allowed to come out into the open and compete for seats in the Parliament. There were many rallies, and I made the mistake of going to one. An old university classmate spotted me. He had also migrated to Cairo, but we had never seen each other until that day at the rally. He was and is a member of the radical arm of the Brotherhood. We had coffee after the rally, and I thought we would go our separate ways. It was not to be."

"How could this man cause you problems?" asked Ken.

"I was finishing a seminar at the University last spring. It had been announced that I was selected to come to the US for this exchange program. This is a prestigious reward, and it got publicity in academic circles. My classmate showed up one afternoon and asked me to join him for coffee. When we arrived at the café, there was another man who joined us."

"Did you know him?" Patrick asked.

"No. He was a stranger. But I soon realized he knew quite a bit about me and the fact I was coming to the US. He was very blunt. He said if I did not assist them in the US, he would disclose my past to the University and the police. They promised to not involve me in any violent activities, but I must assist them as a support person -whatever that was to be. He insisted I not take my family the first year, until I could prove my loyalty to them."

"And that is the reason you didn't bring your family here?"

"Yes. I didn't know what to do, so I agreed to their terms. I fully intended to go back this summer and argue to bring my family here, now that I had been assisting them. I also thought that with the Brotherhood running the government, my past would not be a problem in the future. I didn't count on the military throwing out Marsi and driving the Brotherhood out of government again. It is a mess, but what could I do?

"Had you thought of going to the police?" asked Ken.

"No. It is not like here. No one trusts the police, and they would have tried to get me fired from the University. In fact, the situation is worse now, since we don't know who will take over the government or whether the military will control things like they did in the past."

"Professor, do you know what the two men you brought to Maine are doing there?" asked Patrick.

"I tell you the truth. I do not know and didn't want to know. My objective was to be ignorant if something should happen. It is a coward's way, I know, but I didn't want to be involved. I was, and still am, concerned for my family's safety."

"Did the men say anything about their purpose in going to Maine?" asked Patrick.

"No. In fact, I surmised they were unaware of what they were to do. They had instructions about meeting someone in Portland, but no further information. I did detect from their attitude and their comments that they were radical Jihadists, but I didn't question them."

"Did they tell you much about themselves?" asked Ken.

"No. They said they were students in Canada, at McGill University in Montreal. We talked about the turmoil of the Arab Spring, but I didn't ask them anything about themselves. I was a reluctant courier of these men and didn't want to know anything."

Patrick realized there was much more to discuss with Hakimi, but not tonight. If he were truthful about his contact with the two Jihadists, there was not much more to ask right now. The important objective was to find and neutralize whatever operation these two guys were involved with in Maine.

"We can help you so that no one knows you ever talked or cooperated with us," said Patrick. "We will want to talk again, a number of times, and get specific details from you; but, if you are truthful with us, you will have nothing to fear."

"What about my driving the two men to Maine?"

"All of that can be taken care of, and no one will know of your involvement. The key is truthfulness and cooperation," said Patrick. "If something happens and it comes out that you knew more than you have disclosed here, charges of terrorism would be filed against you - perhaps even murder. That's why I am emphasizing the complete truth of what you know."

"I have told you all I know about these two men and their activities." He looked Patrick straight in the eye as he made that statement. Patrick nodded.

"Will I be able to go home this summer to my family?"

"We will work that out, but I believe it is in both your and our interest that your family joins you here," said Patrick.

"What happens when I am asked to do something again for the Brotherhood?"

"We will discuss how to handle those situations," stated Patrick. "However, from now on, you must tell us immediately when you are contacted, so we can work out a plan that protects you and us."

"Am I to be one of these 007 people? I don't think I am cut out for that kind of intrigue."

"You will be tasked to provide us whatever contact and instructions you receive in the future," said Patrick. "We will work with you to protect your cover. I don't visualize anything dangerous, since the Brotherhood wants to protect you as a support person for them."

Patrick took a plain piece of paper and wrote a telephone number and his first name on it. "I would like you to memorize this telephone number. You can reach me or get a message to me 24 hours a day. If you have any questions or concerns, I want you to call me. Your safety is paramount to me, so long as you are truthful and work with us. I will call you in a couple of days to see how things are going. Just carry out your normal activities and don't worry about cooperating with us. I would offer you a ride home, but we shouldn't be seen together too often. Any questions, Professor?"

"When we again meet, will it be here?"

"No. We will have a quieter and more comfortable place to meet. If someone per chance saw us together today and asks what you were doing, just tell them it was a routine visit by Immigration. ICE makes random contact with legal visa holders, so there should be no suspicion about our meeting. "

They parted company outside the office building, and Patrick and Ken went back to the team house. John Carver was waiting for them there and reported his part of the operation was accomplished without difficulty. The professor had password protected his computer, but John had found the password in a desk drawer in the professor's day planner. "Typical absent-minded professor," said John. He also reported having to evade Dr. Nancy McCray when leaving the area. "She keeps a keen eye for people coming down her street. Someone trained her well."

"You didn't run into her, did you?" asked Patrick.

"No, I used the back entrance and parked down the street. I had a different van and was advertised as a furnace technician. You know everyone gets their furnace cleaned this time of year in New England."

They had arranged to have a late-night secure phone call with Scott Hartley and Doug Foreman to report the results of the interview. After opening cold beers and eating sandwiches John had bought at the local Deli, they made the call.

Patrick and Ken took turns summarizing the interview, and John briefed them on the results of his covert search of the professor's house and computer. A copy of the computer contents was in an overnight mailing to headquarters.

"So, overall, do you believe what he told you tonight?" asked Hartley.

"Yes," said Patrick. "Once we got past the bravado, and he understood we knew things about him, he opened up to us. He got himself in a jam and took the easy way out. If we handle him right, we should have little problem working with him. Ken agrees with my assessment, but Hakimi still is leery of Ken, because of the role he played in the interview."

"Do we need to spend more time with him now?" asked Foreman.

"No, we think the immediate task is to find out what these Jihadists are doing in Maine," said Patrick. "We can wait on all the other details with the Professor. As we thought, he is a support person, and they don't confide their plans to him."

"Okay," said Hartley. "I'll talk with the Bureau and the Police Chief in Portland tomorrow. We need to get this operation out of the closet and see if we can get some new ideas on what is occurring locally there."

"I hope they have some good ideas," said Ken. "We still don't have any intelligence about an operation, except for these two Jihadists going to Portland, Maine. We don't even know if they still are there or left town."

"I hear you," said Foreman. "The thing is, they were met by someone locally and spirited away. We have to assume for now that the pick-up was in Portland because someone locally was used to meet them. Otherwise, they would have gone to Boston or some other large city. If we could identify a suspect for the pick-up, we can follow that trail. Maybe the police or the Bureau has intelligence on a local who fits our needs!"

Hartley asked Patrick and John Carver to be ready to move down to Maine, in case they received any leads from the Bureau or the police. Ken needed to stay in Burlington, since he was conversant with Hakimi, even though Ken was not the professor's favorite special agent. Albert and Bruce would also be ready to move, depending on what occurred the next few days.

Patrick asked if Dick Sandelman could be tasked to especially look for any unusual activity here in New England. Sandelman still wasn't sold on the idea of a terrorist hit in New England, and so Patrick wondered how hard he was researching the intelligence for the area. He mentioned Melissa Wallis, the night supervisor at the DHS Operations Center, who had been supportive of them.

Hartley said he would talk with Sandelman and have Melissa head up the analysis for New England. Business finished, they all signed off for the night.

CHAPTER THIRTY-EIGHT

The four men arrived in Portland from New Jersey in the late afternoon. They signed into the hotel and decided on an early dinner. It had been a somewhat taxing ride, because Dahar and Abdou had driven the cars, getting used to the heavy traffic and American driving habits. All of them were tired from the long day. They did like the location of the hotel and the activity of the Old Port area. Dahar said he wanted to explore the Old Port while they waited for further instructions.

On Thursday, the men wandered along the pathway leading to the East End Beach and the small track railroad that gave rides to tourists. They eventually found themselves in the Back Bay area, taking the long walk around the Bay and ending up at a Hannaford supermarket. They were able to purchase a few personal items, as well as sandwiches and soft drinks, which they later ate while sitting on a bench watching the runners and bikers who used the trails for exercise. Unlike the crowded Old Port, the Back Bay walk gave them exercise and a way to kill time while they waited for instructions. On the way back to the hotel, they stopped and sat on benches along the greenway trail and observed the beachgoers who were sunning on the beach. The remarkable thing they noticed was that no one paid any particular attention to them. Unlike most of the state, Portland has a very diverse population, and for them to see women in Muslim garb, strolling along with children, was a complete surprise. They also were able to find a restaurant that evening serving Middle Eastern food.

On Friday, Umar and Awad had to arrange a meeting with Ben and the two Jihadists who were staying out at the farm. The purpose was to give them the two cars they had brought up from New Jersey. They located the meeting place on a map of the local area. The transfer was to take place at about 3:30 in the afternoon. Dahar wanted to see the Old Port, and it was decided that Abdou should accompany him, since it was believed to be safer traveling in pairs. None of the men really knew the area, and it appeared from their drive around Portland last evening that some places along the waterfront looked a bit rough. They also saw men with loud motorcycles and lots of tattoos.

Both Abdou and Dahar started off on their sightseeing after Umar and Awad left for the vehicle transfer. The desk clerk had given them a map of the area and suggested a route they could take to see all the sights of the Old Port area. They passed the ferry terminal, where boats took tourists and residents out to the various islands in Casco Bay. Dahar pointed out that this would be a good day outing for the four men. Abdou said little except to comment on the dress of the women. It was a hot day, and people were dressed in summer casual: shorts, bathing suits, and low-cut summer dresses. While Abdou made derogatory comments as they passed scantily- dressed women, Dahar noticed that Abdou made sure he looked each one of them over very carefully - even to the point of rudeness!

They had walked slowly, observing the sights for over an hour, when Dahar suggested they stop somewhere for a drink, since he was thirsty. Most all the establishments serving drinks were bars, but they knew they could order non-alcoholic drinks, too. It was getting on towards five o'clock, and the crowds were growing: tourists, people getting off from work, and passengers from a large cruise ship that was docked at the port.

Dahar spotted a place called *Babes & Bikes* and suggested they stop there. The door was open, and they could smell the aroma of beer, but the bar didn't appear to be any worse or better than what they had seen on their walk. It was somewhat dark inside, but they strolled in, looking to find a place to sit. There was a long bar along the right side of the room that was crowded, with every seat occupied and people standing behind them. They thought it better to find a table, rather than compete with all the customers crowding the bar. All the tables near the front of the establishment were filled, so they strolled towards the rear of the room. The tables there appeared occupied, too, and so they started back towards the front. As they passed one table, they noticed two women sitting there, but there were also two empty chairs. One of the women noticed them, because she called out, "You two handsome guys looking for a seat?"

Abdou seemed startled, since he was not accustomed to women seeking him out, but Dahar smiled and looked at the two women. "Come on and sit," she said. "There ain't any other empty chairs. It's Friday, and everyone is out for a good time." Both women were not what one would call beautiful, but they were good-looking with a sexy demeanor. Both had short, dark hair and wore tight jeans and low-cut blouses. The woman who spoke was the taller of the two, but both looked like they worked out or were into physical exercise. They appeared to be in their mid- 20's, the same age range as the two men. Daher looked at Abdou and indicated they should sit.

"Thank you. You are very kind," Dahar said. "We were thirsty and wanted to just come in for a refreshing drink."

"Well, you've come to the right place. They have crazy drinks here, and they are real good. By the way, my name is Terri, and this is my best friend, Tammy."

"Oh, hello, Terri and Tammy. My name is Dahar, and this is my friend Abdou." He used their family names instead of their first names, because that's how they addressed each other since arriving in the US. Also, he didn't think these women would know the difference.

"You guys live here or just visiting?" asked Terri.

"We are just traveling through on our way back to St. Maarten," said Dahar. "We were at a culinary meeting in Rhode Island and thought we would see Portland, too."

"So you guys are chefs," said Tammy.

"Yes, we work in the food business," said Abdou. He appeared uncomfortable sitting with the two women, but Dahar noticed he was focused on their low-cut blouses and ample breasts. Dahar noticed that both women had identical small tattoos on their arms and a number of rings on the fingers of both hands. At that moment, a waitress came by and asked about drinks. The women asked for refills of their drinks.

Abdou said he wanted a cola, but Tammy said he should try the Friday cola special. He shrugged and said okay.

Dahar noticed the orange juice that Terri was drinking and said he wanted a large orange drink like Terri's.

The bar was hot and noisy, and a DJ was playing music on a raised platform near the back of the room by the toilets. There was a small area for dancing, and it was crowded: mostly tourists. The women were talkative and plied both men with questions about St. Maarten. To be polite, Dahar responded to their questions, but Abdou seemed disinterested, except to leer at the women's breasts. They had received their drinks, and Dahar really enjoyed his orange juice. In fact, at Terri's suggestion, Dahar

Francis Dillon

immediately ordered another round of drinks, because the waitress was so busy serving other tables. Abdou seemed to just sip his drink, because the cola had a strong flavor he couldn't place.

After his second orange juice, Dahar asked the women about the meaning of the tattoos. Each had a small heart with what looked like a skull in the center with a small cross over the skull.

Both women laughed, and Terri said, "We are members of a motorcycle club. It's called the *Casco Bay Riders.*"

"Is this just a women's club?" Dahar asked.

"No, it's both men and women," said Terri. "We travel around the state together. In fact, several people in here now are members. This is sort of our home bar, where we gather before rides. You saw the name of this place, didn't you? We are riding down to Old Orchard Beach later tonight, after everyone gets here. Do you ride motorcycles?"

"No," said Dahar "We just came in here to get a drink. We don't know anything about motorcycles. What does that skull and cross mean? Is it your recognition symbol?"

"Yeah, I guess you could call it that," said Terri. "The skull indicates we are dare-devil riders, and the cross is our protection when we do dangerous things. Someone thought that up years ago after we had too many drinks, and so it has become our thing."

When the waitress served them another round of drinks, Dahar noticed everyone was keeping pace except Abdou. He still was on his first drink and added little to the conversation.

222

Dahar felt "great" and didn't flinch but was shocked when Terri suggested they dance.

"I don't know how to dance," he said.

"Oh, that doesn't matter," she said. "There's not much room to move back there, but I love to dance after I've had a few orange juices. Come on, I'll show you."

To be polite, Dahar stood and followed her to the back of the room. There was still a crowd of dancers, and he felt somewhat hemmed in when Terri put her arms around his shoulders and cuddled in close. "Just move easy back and forth," she murmured. "The music is slow and dreamy and easy to relax with. We don't have to move around too much."

Dahar couldn't move very far if he wanted to, given the crush of the crowd in this small space. He felt Terri's breast against his chest and her pleasant scent as she held him close. Although he had some experience with women he had never danced before. This new experience caused physical arousal, and he wondered what would occur next. The music stopped, but they both were still locked together. Dahar enjoyed it but didn't know what to do. The music started again, a slow piece, and Terri whispered in his ear, "Let's just stay here while the music is so dreamy." She kissed him on the ear and he nestled his head against hers.

After the third dance, the beat picked up, and Terri suggested they sit until a dreamy set of music started again. Dahar was by now enjoying the experience but agreed, since he had no idea what to do. When the fast music started, people came apart, swinging each other around. There was no cuddling with this dance music. As they started back to the table, a very tall and muscular male appeared. He was dressed in jeans and a tight black tee shirt. He had a large belt around his waist with small chains on it. He stopped them both short by holding his left hand out, almost putting his fingers in Dahar's face.

"Ray," Terri said. "I didn't know you were coming with us this evening."

"Well, I am. I traded places at work. Now, who is this guy?" as he pointed to Dahar. "You start running around when you don't think I'll be here, Terri?"

"Listen, Ray, I just had a dance with this fellow to be friendly. He and his friend are here from St. Maarten. We were just having a couple drinks while we waited for the gang to gather here. They are moving on soon."

"Oh, yeah. I saw you on the dance floor. You trying to move in my girl, buddy?"

At first, Dahar didn't know what to say, but, having grown up in Marseilles, he'd learned to hold his own at an early age, and this fellow didn't scare him. "I was just being polite and danced with this young lady," he said. "She and her friend were kind to offer us a seat so we could have a cold beverage. My name is Dahar, and you haven't introduced yourself."

"I don't need to introduce myself, buddy. I saw you snuggling up to my girl here, and I don't put up with that stuff."

"I don't know what you mean, but Terri just asked me to dance, and, to be polite, I accepted. Is there something wrong with that?"

"Yeah, there is. I saw you out there. That was no polite dance. You were making a move on her."

"I don't know what you mean by that, but you seem very angry over nothing."

"Listen, you snake, you know very well what you were doing to her." His voice was raised, and, as he talked louder, the bar seemed to get quieter. He also grabbed Terri's arm and told her to go sit down. She started to protest and he pushed her towards the table. She fell over a chair, and as she got up, he pushed her again towards the table.

"Please don't do that to her," said Dahar. "She has done nothing wrong."

"If you don't shut up, I am going to push you, too... right out the door." Ray moved closer to Dahar to emphasize his intention, but Dahar didn't budge. The patrons began to move away, and the music from the DJ's perch also stopped.

They stood glaring at one another, and, before the manager could approach from behind the bar to separate them, Ray started to take a swing at Dahar. While he was a big man, he wasn't very agile, and Dahar stepped back as he saw Ray move his shoulder back to swing at him. The punch went into the air in front of Dahar. Ray glared and moved into Dahar to punish him with his fists. The manager motioned to one of the bartenders to call the police. In the past, the bar had a reputation for fights, and the new owners worked hard to cater to tourists and build some rapport with the police.

While Dahar took one glancing punch to the face, he twirled around, and ducked, while at the same time coming up with a six-inch blade knife that he kept in an ankle pouch. He ran the blade across Ray's knuckles, spurting blood. Ray recoiled from the sting of the blade, and Dahar followed up with a slash across his face. Ray had a cut from near his right eye to his chin. He bellowed and fell towards the floor, as Dahar kneed him in the groin. As the big man fell in pain, two of the larger bartenders grabbed Dahar from behind, locking his arms and hands, while the manager shouted to him to drop the knife.

At that moment, two Portland police officers rushed into the bar. On most evenings, and especially on weekends, there is always extra police presence in the Old Port. These two officers were walking just down the street from the *Babes and Bikes* bar when they received the call from their dispatch center. On entering, one of the officers saw the knife in Dahar's hand. With no hesitation, he pulled his tazer weapon and fired it at Dahar. The shock caused him to drop the knife and fall to the floor. They quickly cuffed Dahar and called for backup and an ambulance for Ray.

Abdou, who had been watching all this action, was shocked and a bit frightened. Although he was a committed Jihadist, he had never been in personal fights like this. He stood up from the table and moved discreetly towards the door. The attention of the patrons was directed at Ray and Dahar, so Abdou was able to move unnoticed by the crowd. Tammy was busy consoling Terri. When he saw Dahar draw a knife, he left the bar and crossed the street, standing in a doorway of a closed store. He saw the police arrive, and later the follow-on police van and ambulance. He waited until Dahar was escorted out of the bar and into the police van. As the vehicle drove away, he headed quickly back to the hotel.

Umar and Awad had returned earlier to the hotel and were waiting for Dahar and Abdou to return to go to dinner. Abdou found them in their room and relayed the events that he had witnessed.

"So they arrested Dahar?" asked Umar.

"They took him away in a police van in handcuffs. The other guy was taken away in an ambulance. Many of the patrons left the bar and I heard them talking about the big guy getting knifed by Dahar. So they probably are going to put Dahar in jail."

"We can't stay here," said Awad. "They will search and question him and then come here once they know he is staying in a hotel."

"We don't have a car any longer," said Umar. "We need to check out now and call a taxi to take us to the airport."

"Yes, but the police will be able to trace us to the airport," said Awad.

"I know. But hopefully the police will assume we went to the airport to fly away. But, once we get to the airport, I will rent a car, and we will go to a hotel in a town close by to here. Abdou, go pack both your and Dahar's belongings and meet us in the lobby. I'll tell the desk clerk we have an emergency at home and must fly out of Portland tonight."

"What about Aarif?" said Awad.

"I'll call him once we get to another hotel," said Umar. "We can't make plans to meet him until we have our new location. Right now, we must get away quickly before the police come here."

"What about Dahar?" asked Abdou.

"We just have to leave him," said Umar. "We have no choice. He is a Jihadist. He won't tell the police anything. This is a problem for Aarif to resolve."

CHAPTER THIRTY-NINE

Patrick and John Carver had driven to Maine on Friday and stayed at Patrick's summer home in Bath. They were to await a telephone call from Scott Hartley, who was to contact the Bureau and the Portland Police Chief. After the necessary arrangements had been made, Hartley wanted Patrick and John to brief both agencies and see what leads could be developed. Hartley had concerns that the FBI resident agent in Portland could be a problem if he wanted to assert the Bureau's jurisdiction in the matter. Fortunately, the local FBI office was swamped with work, and Hartley was able to convince him that Homeland Security still didn't have a definite lead that anything was going to occur in the Portland area. The Police Chief, Mark Daniels, was cooperative and said his department would gladly help, so long as "the Feds" didn't hold back any information. Like most police chiefs today, he wouldn't put up with that "big brother knows best attitude" that was so prevalent in the past from federal agents, especially the FBI. The Chief also suggested that a representative from the Sheriff's office and the State Police be included, since his department's jurisdiction was limited to the city. Hartley thought that idea made sense and asked Daniels for the names of people he should call at both agencies. It was agreed that they would initially set up a command post for the operation at the police department.

Around 6:00, Friday evening, Hartley called Patrick and told him of his talk with Chief Daniels, and that the Sheriff's office and State Police would be part of their task force. He advised that he had arranged for Patrick and John to brief the agencies together on Monday morning at the Portland police station. While Hartley wanted to move faster, he knew the two other departments would need some time to decide who was going to represent them. DHS didn't have any specific leads to pursue in Maine, unless the meeting produced new information. He also didn't want to make the "locals" feel like they were being pushed by the Feds.

Depending on the results of their Monday meeting, Hartley told Patrick he would move Ken, Bruce, and Albert down from Burlington, since they had little to do up there at this time. The contact telephone number they had given Professor Hakimi was a cell phone, so it didn't matter where the team was located. If Hakimi called, they could fly someone back to Burlington. They discussed a few more logistic issues, and then Hartley rung off.

It was mid-morning on Saturday and Patrick and John were sitting on Patrick's deck enjoying the summer air. They both were drinking coffee and reading the morning's papers. They talked about going out on Patrick's boat to do some striper fishing, since they had no work to do until Monday. Patrick's wife was away visiting grandchildren, and Patrick told John he would show him some of the area's fine restaurants this weekend. They also talked about watching a Portland Sea Dogs game on Sunday. The Sea Dogs were a AA farm team of the Boston Red Sox, and many of the current Red Sox players had played with the Sea Dogs. However, their leisure plans were interrupted by a call from Scott Hartley on Patrick's secure telephone line. Patrick put the phone on speaker mode so John could participate, too.

"Sorry to bother you guys," said Scott, "but Melissa Wallis spotted an arrest up in Portland last evening, and she and Nola Hunter have pulled together a lot of good information this morning. I think we have some serious leads to follow up on, and we need to do it today. Melissa has been up all night, since she is the night supervisor in the Operations Center, but I wanted her here for this phone call before I send her home to sleep. I'll have Melissa tell you what she found, and then Nola will follow up with her work this morning."

"I know we haven't met," said Melissa, "but Nola has told me so much about you guys, I feel like I know you."

"The feeling is mutual," said Patrick. "When this operation is over, we'll all have a get-together. Right now, John and I are ready to take notes, and then you can go home and get some sleep."

"Okay. Last night, one of the new analysts whom Nola has been training showed me a report she spotted on the wire. It was a report about a fight in a bar in Portland and the arrest of a foreign national. We don't usually get such reports, but the local police sometimes send them to us when foreigners from the Middle East are involved. In this case, the Subject, Samir Dahar, was arrested for stabbing another male in a bar fight. He had a French passport and driver's license, but looked like someone from the Middle East, probably a French Algerian. He wouldn't talk with the police, but, when they searched him, they found a key for a local hotel. When they checked with the hotel, they discovered he was staying there with three other males who also looked to be Middle Eastern. These three men had abruptly left the hotel about 7:00 Friday evening, saying they had an emergency at home. They appeared to have taken Dahar's belongings with them."

"I wonder how the three men knew Dahar had been arrested?" asked John.

"Well, the report further said that Dahar was in the bar with a friend who left before the police arrived. The police surmise that one of the three guys that left the hotel was with

Dahar and went to the hotel to alert the others after Dahar was arrested."

"Did the hotel clerk know where these guys were headed when they departed the hotel?" asked Patrick.

"Well, that's the funny part. When they arrived a few days ago, they had two cars, but, when they left the hotel last night, they asked the desk clerk to get them a taxi. I assume the police may follow up on that," said Melissa. "Now let me have Nola tell you what she discovered."

"Hi guys. Hope you are enjoying the Maine weather," said Nola. "It's already too hot here, so I'm ready to come to Portland."

"What are you doing there on a Saturday morning?" asked Patrick. "I thought you were just training people during the week."

"Well, I am, but I have to train the new analysts on the night shift, too. So I come in around 5:00 AM and see what they have been doing all night, and then we discuss their work. It helps Melissa, since she has a lot of other responsibilities, and we all work well together. My Mom took the kids to the beach for the weekend, so I thought I'd get in a little training with the night shift crew this weekend."

"I'm glad she did," said Melissa. "She has been great working with me this morning, especially since she had some sleep before she got here."

"Sounds good to me," said Patrick, "and let's hear Nola's information."

"I took the four names that Melissa gave me and ran them through the Customs Immigration database. Both Samir Dahar and Rabiah Abdou arrived here just the other day from the island of St. Maarten. Dahar has a French passport, and Abdou has a Dutch passport. Both said they were going to a culinary conference at Johnson and Wales University in Providence, Rhode Island, and would only be here a week. Each gave his residence as the University. However, when I checked this morning, the University said there was no such conference and never heard of these guys."

"What about the other two?" asked John.

"They are brothers, Umar and Awad Hussein. They are here on student visas, but should have gone home several months ago. Of course, no one checks on these people, and, until they showed up in the police report, the authorities had no idea whether they were still in the country or gone home."

"Is there any intelligence information on these guys?" asked Patrick.

"Yes," said Nola. "The brothers are from Yemen and did undergraduate studies in the UK. When they applied here to study at the Wharton Business School, ICE did a records check with the Brits. MI5 sent a report back that the brothers were known Jihadist sympathizers and had attended meetings sponsored by a radical Imam, but they had not participated in any known illegal activities. They have been here a year and a half and have no police record, except they should have gone home last January."

"It is very strange that the brothers joined up with these two guys from St. Maarten and they all came to Portland," said Hartley.

"Do we know anything about the two guys from St. Maarten?" asked John.

"Not yet," said Hartley. "We are sending out requests now to both the French and the Dutch, and also Interpol. Since St. Maarten is a divided island between the French and Dutch, we will check locally and back in their home countries. I want to call Chief Daniels, but first wanted to speak with you both about our next move. According to the police report, Dahar isn't talking to the police, and I imagine they will have to appoint a lawyer for him. It would be good if we could interview him and see if he would talk to us. I don't want to insult the police, but we do have information they don't have, and we could make some type of deal with him if he would talk. You have any thoughts?"

"Yes," said Patrick. "Scott, do you know a fellow by the name of Ayman Siede?"

"That name isn't familiar. Why are you mentioning him?"

"Nola and I have used him to assist several clients who are involved in business in the Middle East. He comes from Lebanon, and his father was a language professor at the American University in Beirut. His mother is also Lebanese but was brought up in the US. Ayman went to college in Boston, and his family eventually moved here because Hezbollah was threatening his father. Ayman speaks several languages and has worked for the CIA and possibly the FBI, too, as a contractor."

"He sounds like a good guy, but how is he of help to us?"

"Well, Scott, I have an idea. Ayman is the president of some American/Muslim relations group. For all I know, he may be the only member, but he has used this group's name to get information. For example, he told me one time he got information out of a guy the CIA was targeting. He used his position in this American/Muslim group to befriend the guy, got the guy to talk, and also helped the guy out with some legal problems. The result was the guy never knew Ayman was working for the CIA, Ayman got the information the CIA wanted, and the guy thought Ayman was a prince of a fellow because he helped him with his legal issues."

"OK, said Hartley, "but how does this help us with Dahar in the Portland jail?"

"I'll have to talk with Ayman, but listen to this scenario. Dahar knows he is in trouble over the bar fight. But he doesn't know we are on to him. What if Siede talks with Dahar, tells him he is there to help a fellow Muslim. He scares him, saying the federal authorities know he lied about his purpose in coming to the US, and that Dahar needs to tell Ayman everything so he can help him before the Feds arrive; otherwise, the Feds could send him to Guantanamo or some other place."

"That's a nice story, Patrick, but how would Siede know about the federal issue? He can't say he works for the government."

"Scott, when you meet Siede, you'll see what he can do. Remember when we were kids and people used to comment about a smooth guy being one who could sell refrigerators to the Eskimos? Well, Ayman is that type of guy. He will spin some sort of story about his organization having sources in the government and all that nonsense."

"Patrick's right about Ayman Siede," said Nola. "I have seen him deal with some tough issues for our clients, and he is good. Also, if he doesn't think he can solve your problem, he will tell you. Unless anyone has some other thoughts on how we can get Dahar to talk, I don't see we have much choice."

They discussed a few other ideas, but everyone concluded that the Ayman Siede scenario could be their best option at this point. Scott Hartley told Patrick to contact Siede and see if he could assist them. In the meantime, Hartley would call Chief Daniels and see if they could track down the Hussein brothers and Rabiah Abdou, but not to take them into custody or talk with them. Hartley would also tell Daniels of the possible interview with Dahar using Siede and to not allow Dahar to post bond and leave jail.

"How can the police chief keep him in jail if his lawyer posts bond?" asked John.

"I'll ask Chief Daniels to tell the prosecutor that we regard Dahar as a flight risk and that we want to talk with him about lying as to his purpose in being here in the US," said Hartley. "Once the judge knows the Feds are going to serve a terrorist type warrant, he won't let him go."

"I'm sure the locals will have to appoint a lawyer for Dahar," said Patrick. "Will there be any problems having to go through the lawyer to talk with Dahar?"

"I don't think so," said Hartley. "Your friend Siede is going to visit a fellow Muslim to help him out. If Siede gets any information from Dahar that concerns him, Siede can always tell us about the information, as any good citizen would do. I'll talk to Daniels about that, too. Since it is the weekend, they probably won't arraign him until Monday. If he hasn't already asked for a lawyer, he won't get one appointed until the arraignment. Patrick, let me know about your contact with Siede, and we'll get moving here today."

CHAPTER FORTY

Rabiah Abdou and Umar and Awad Hussein took a taxi from the hotel to the Portland Jetport. On arrival, Umar told the driver to let them out at the United Airlines doorway. They entered the terminal and, instead of going up to the passenger counter, headed down to the baggage area. While waiting for the taxi in Portland, they discussed staying at an airport hotel rather than renting a car that evening. They concluded their physical appearance would draw less attention at the international airport and believed it would be more secure to stay there for the night. They would then telephone Aarif and discuss what they should do.

Upon entering the baggage area, they saw a bank of telephones advertising hotels and restaurants. Umar was about to call a hotel when they saw a large van from the Hilton Garden airport hotel pull up to the door. Several people were waiting for it, and so they joined the queue. Upon arriving at the hotel, they were able to book three rooms with no noticeable scrutiny from the desk clerk. After settling in, they gathered in Umar's room while he contacted Aarif.

Umar proceeded to tell Aarif of the incident involving Samir Dahar and his arrest. At the mention of arrest, Umar had to hold the phone away from his ear, as Aarif began shouting at him and yelling that this could wreck the operation. Umar listened to this harangue for a couple of minutes and finally was able to speak.

"Aarif, we can't do anything about the incident. It occurred, and now we have to make other plans. Tell me, what do you want us to do?"

Umar listened to Aarif spout off for another couple of minutes, and then the telephone call ended. "He is going to talk with Ben and then call us back," said Umar. "I don't think Aarif reacts well when he is faced with unexpected problems like this."

"Did he have any thoughts about what we should do?" asked Abdou.

"No, he just ranted on about ruining his operation."

Upon ending the phone call from Umar, Aarif tore out of his room and began shouting for Ben. He found him sitting on the front porch by himself, gazing at the night sky. Apparently, Destiny had gone to bed.

"Ben, Ben, we have big problems," said Aarif. "That stupid driver from St. Maarten, Samir Dahar, went into a bar, got into a fight, and is now in jail. We have to do something so we don't wreck our plans."

"Calm down, Aarif, and tell me what happened. We can't do anything until we have a few facts. Where are the others? Did they vacate the hotel in Portland?"

"Yes, yes, they left the hotel in Portland and are now at a hotel at the airport. I need to call Umar back and tell them what to do. How are we going to get Dahar out of jail? We don't want him talking to the police."

"Let me call Umar and get some more information while you calm down." Ben dialed the phone number Aarif gave him and listened to Umar describe what had happened. Ben had put the cell phone on the speaker mode so Aarif could also hear the conversation. Abdou then got on the phone and described how they happened to go into the bar, the women they met, and the fight. He told him that the situation might be very serious, because the other guy had been taken away in an ambulance with several stab wounds. Abdou said he didn't know Dahar that well, only meeting him two days ago, but believed he wouldn't say anything to the police about the operation.

"While Dahar doesn't know details, it would be best if he didn't talk at all to the police, since they would ask him what he was doing in Portland," said Ben. "We will just have to leave him on his own, since I don't see how any of us can go to the jail in Portland. We can't even get him a lawyer, because that would raise questions."

"Can we take the chance that he won't talk?" asked Aarif.

"We have to," said Ben. "We have come too far to stop now. All we need are a couple of days, and then we can clear out of here and send the drivers to their target locations. Umar, I will pick you all up in the morning and bring you here. It will be safer. We can then make final decisions as to when we leave here."

They concluded the conversation, and Ben told Aarif to go to bed and get some rest. "It won't help for you to be upset and emotional," he said. "You need to be calm and positive around the others; otherwise, they will begin to have doubts about our plan and worry too. We need everyone to focus on their part of this plan. We can do this, Aarif; just get yourself together, and we will work everything out in the morning."

Aarif looked at Ben and said he would be okay in the morning. Ben wondered if Aarif wasn't more concerned about what the sponsors of this operation would think of him if their plan failed, rather than the brothers who volunteered for this suicide operation. Despite his demeanor as an Imam and local leader, Aarif definitely was not a crisis manager.

As he entered their bedroom, Ben saw that Destiny was awake and reading a book. He also noticed the open window that was above the porch where he had been sitting. "I see your buddy has another crisis on his hands," said Destiny.

"Were you listening to us?"

"I couldn't help but hear you, with all the screaming by Josef. Oh, I heard you call him by another name, a foreign name. What's the story? Is Josef not his name?"

"He goes by two names. He prefers Josef around non-Muslims, but goes by Aarif when we speak privately."

"Oh, a man of mystery. What else should I know about him, Ben? After all I have done for you guys, I'm not privy to know things? I am fed up with your kooky friends here, Ben, and now I overheard you and Josef, or whatever his name is, are going to bring some more of them here."

"Listen, Destiny, I'm sorry about Josef's name issue. I didn't mean to keep things from you. And, yes, we need to bring three more men here tomorrow; but it will just be for a couple of days, and then we all will be out of here."

"Why can't they stay downtown?"

"It's complicated. One of the guys got into a bar fight and was sent to jail. The others need to come here, because it is safer. We only have a couple more days until the operation. I'll keep them out of your way, okay?"

"Ben, why do we have all these foreigners here? Why couldn't you get some of your friends from the mosque down in New Jersey and have them drive these cars up to the federal buildings? Is there something else you haven't told me? You are just going to bomb these empty buildings over the 4th of July, aren't you?"

"Calm down, Destiny. That's our plan, the federal buildings. We had to get people from out of the country, because they are unknown to the cops. If we used local guys from our mosque, there is a big risk that somehow they could be identified. We had the money, so we decided to get foreign guys."

"Well, you probably could have got people from the west coast to do the driving. But I don't care, just get everybody out of here, before my friends find out who's here."

"We plan to leave in two days at the latest. I told Josef that we should send the drivers out early, so they can get to their assigned cities and scout out the buildings before the 4th. It will work fine, and no one will know they came from here."

"What if these foreign guys get lost or picked up by the cops?"

"That's not a problem. They don't know where they are, except for being in Maine. If stopped and questioned, they will say they were paid by a local stranger to drive a car to an address of a federal building, and leave it there. They agreed, because they needed money, and the stranger paid them up-front to drive the car. They won't mention being up here at all."

"How do you know you can trust them? If the cops threaten them, they could tell them everything. I've been thinking about this for the past two weeks. If you guys screw this up, it could jeopardize my getting a law license."

"Destiny, don't worry. Our plan is good. These guys won't talk to the cops or the Feds, or anyone else. They are being paid well and know the risks."

This conversation went on for another half hour, Destiny bringing up problems and Ben trying to convince her that their plan would work and she would never be connected to it. Destiny fell off to sleep still worrying that Ben wasn't telling her everything about their plan. She decided to talk with Ghanem when Ben was not around and see what he had to say.

CHAPTER FORTY-ONE

Patrick was fortunate. He sent Ayman Siede a text message to call him, on a secure phone if possible, because he had an urgent need for his services. Ayman called him within the hour.

"Patrick, I just looked at my iPhone and saw your text message. I was at my grandson's baseball game and had left my phone at home so I wouldn't be disturbed. These games are important, you know."

"Oh, I agree Ayman, The kids grow up quickly, so you need to enjoy them while you can. How are you? I haven't talked with you in months."

"I'm doing well and hope to spend most of the summer at home with the family. But your message said you have an urgent problem. I hope this isn't going to involve a lot of traveling?"

"No. In fact I just need you to come up to Portland for a day at the most and help me with an interview."

"That, I can do for you. In fact, I can then bring some fresh lobster home to the family. Now, what's the problem that requires my immediate attention?"

Patrick proceeded to brief him on the situation and what he would like Ayman to do for him. They discussed what kind of role Ayman could play to get this Samir Dahar to confide in him. There were several possibilities, but Ayman recalled a scenario he used on a CIA case and thought it might work with Dahar. They agreed to meet Sunday morning at the police station and go over the final details. Patrick would check with Hartley and then contact Chief Daniels directly so they could set up a time for Ayman to talk with Dahar.

᪶

Sunday afternoon, Dahar was led into an interview room in the Portland jail. He looked defiant as he entered and was cuffed to a chair. He then looked at the stranger sitting across from him and seemed somewhat confused. "Who are you?"

"A friend," said Ayman. "Officer, you may uncuff him as you leave us. We will be all right. We are just going to chat for a while."

"Okay," said the guard, "but I will be sitting outside this room. Call out when you need me."

When the guard left the room, Ayman said in French, "My name is Ayman. I am a fellow Muslim, and I am here to assist you."

"Are you a lawyer?" replied Dahar, also in French.

"No, but I can help you with your problem. A judge will assign you a lawyer when they take you to court on Monday. For privacy sake, we will continue speaking French. No one is recording our conversation, but I don't want the guard to hear what we say."

"Okay, but how can you help me? Who sent you here?"

"I am going to tell you about our organization and how we can help you. It will take a few minutes. You know how our brothers hit the Americans on 9/11?"

Dahar nodded but didn't say anything.

"Well, after things calmed down, the Americans decided they needed to have more information about our people here in this country. A few of us believers decided to form a group and appear to assist the Americans. We call ourselves The Muslim-American Friendship Group."

"Do you really help them?"

"Not really, but it gives us great influence with the American authorities. We tell them things that are going on in our community, but really nothing important. Occasionally, we give them names of 'hotheads' who we can't control, and that helps our credibility. In return, we have gained insight into how they are targeting our brothers. We also have been able to get some sources in their government. There are always Americans who will tell you things for the right amount of money."

"How does that help me?"

"We found out you were here from a source. Now you have to give me information so I can help you."

"What kind of information?"

"I assume you are not a resident here. Is that correct?"

"Yes. I came from St. Maarten. I am a visitor."

"What did you tell the Immigration people when you arrived?"

"I said I was going to a cooking class at a school in Rhode Island."

"Yes, but you are here in Portland. Were you really to go to this cooking school?"

"Well, no, but that's what I was told to tell them."

"So, I assume you are in Portland for something else?"

Dahar seemed to stiffen his body and said, "Why do you ask me that? How can that information help me?"

Ben smiled at him, and lowered his voice. "Dahar, please don't be angry with me. I can help you, but let me explain. Because you are not a resident, we know the police will check with the federal authorities. When they find out you are supposed to be in Rhode Island and instead you are in Portland, they will notify the FBI. Do you know what that means?"

"No, but I won't tell them anything. They can go to hell!"

"Please calm down and listen. If some sort of attack occurs here and you gave a false story of where you were going in the United States, they will assume you were to be part of the operation. Then the Homeland Security laws will allow them to treat you as a terrorist and not a criminal. Do you know what that means?"

"I don't care. I won't talk to them. They can't make me talk. I read that in the newspaper."

"It has nothing to do with you talking. The law allows them to put you away and keep you there forever."

"That's not possible. The brothers told me there are laws here."

"The brothers misinformed you. It's possible you will spend the rest of your life in a federal prison after the police are finished with you here. You made a grave mistake. Stabbing a man in a bar over a woman was not the way to support our cause. You should have been preparing yourself as a Jihadist who is about to do battle with the enemy. If you want to make up for offending Allah, you need to talk to me, and then we will see how we can help you."

Ayman then sat back and said nothing. Dahar stared at the floor. This silence went on for at least 3 or 4 minutes with neither man speaking. Ayman was used to this posture. He had found over the years that silence often caused reflection, and that, in turn, most often led to a conversation. Ayman quietly opened his copy of the Koran and began reading silently.

Suddenly, Dahar began to sob but said nothing.

Ayman noticed him but did not speak. Dahar's sobbing became louder and he began to rock back in forth in the chair. Tears rolled down his cheeks and onto his jail uniform. Ayman finally leaned over and gave him a handkerchief and resumed reading his Koran. After a while, Dahar ceased crying and gradually stopped rocking in his chair. His head was down, and he looked lost in thought. After several more minutes, Ayman said, "You are obviously conflicted. How can I help you?"

"I don't think you or anyone else can help me," said Dahar as he spoke with a tremble in his voice.

"I have years of experience helping people, so maybe I can help you."

"Are you a doctor?"

"No, but I have trained as a counselor and I know from experience that talking out your problem with someone can be helpful in finding a solution."

"I don't think there is a solution. You say the authorities can lock me up. Yet I can't complete my mission. What will my family think? I am a failure." He continued to hang down his head and not look directly at Ayman.

"Dahar, did you come on this mission for yourself or to prove something to your family?"

"You don't know what it is like to be the youngest son in a large family." He raised his head and looked directly at Ayman. His voice became stronger. "I was raised in a family of bakers. My father has the largest Muslim bakery in Marseille. My two older brothers help my father run the bakery now. When I came of age, my father told me there was no room for me in the business. He sent me to the Brotherhood. They sent me off to the training camps. I wasn't really excited about this training, but what was I to do?"

"Did you ask your father to help you start a different business, perhaps a restaurant or something?"

"You don't know my father. He is very conservative, and he has many friends who have sons in the Brotherhood. So he sent me to them so he could also brag to his friends that we now have a Jihadist in the family."

"So the Brotherhood sent you here?"

"Not directly. They sent me to St. Maarten and told me to get a job there. They would contact me when they needed me."

"So what did you do there?"

"I was raised in a baker family, and I know the business. I was lucky. There is this older French couple who have a nice bakery business in the Orient Beach area. I went there one morning for breakfast and found out they were looking for a baker to help them. I told them about my family experience, and they hired me. I have been with them for almost 10 months. In fact, we talked about me buying the bakery from them in a year or two when they want to retire. We get along real well. They have no children and treat me like a son. I really like it there."

"What would prevent you from going back after your mission?"

"You don't understand, Mr. Ayman. I was so happy with my work, and then I met a *lady of the book*. She is older than me and well educated. She designs jewelry and sells it to the tourists on the beach. I met her because she came into the bakery every day for coffee. We started talking, and soon we started getting together after work."

"This woman is a Christian?"

"Yes, but she is different than the infidels I have met in France. We have had very deep discussions about all sorts of religions. She has studied these subjects in college, but now prefers her present life. I even went with her to a church one Sunday. Oh, I shouldn't tell you these things!"

"No, that's okay. Despite what the Brotherhood preaches, it is good for us Muslims to understand other cultures. Your *lady of the book* sounds like a fine woman."

"Oh, she is, she is. We even started living together. I have never had such a relationship with a female before."

"What did you tell her and your employer when you left the island?"

"Oh, that was very difficult. I didn't know what to do, but the Brotherhood told me to say that I had to go home for a few weeks to France because of a family illness. I did that, but it was hard to tell a lie to people you like and trust."

"Well, how did the Brotherhood give you instructions? Did they contact you directly?"

"No, they are not on St. Maarten. When they sent me to the Island, I was instructed to check this web site every week, and it would have orders when they wanted me to do something. I almost forgot about it as time went by. In fact, I was so happy with my life there that I hoped that they would forget about me."

"But you did check the web site, as they instructed you?"

"Well, yes, because I also got news of my family from this web site."

"Does your family know of your lady friend?"

"No. I don't communicate very often with them. I was only close with my mother, and she died last year. My father would never understand my relationship with this woman. I have a sister I write to occasionally. My brothers could care less about me."

As Ayman continued to engage Dahar with questions, his demeanor changed. He became less suspicious of Ayman and actually seemed to be telling him things that had been weighing on his mind. Ayman kept his conversation light, gathering information about Dahar's life on St. Maarten and hoping to gradually get him to talk about his mission.

"Would you like to go back to your job and your lady friend on St. Maarten?" asked Ayman.

"That has been in my thoughts as I sat here in jail this past day. But I have my family's honor to uphold. How can I not carry out my mission?"

"Well, really, you can't go anywhere now, so there won't be any mission for you."

"Yes, but how do I explain this to my family?"

"It appears, Samir Dahar, that your family abandoned you when they sent you to St. Maarten. And now you have made a new life for yourself, a life that has brought you happiness."

"Yes, but what about my father? How can he brag to his friends about his son the Jihadist when I am here and can't do my mission?"

"If you are only doing a mission so your father can boast to his friends, I would say your father doesn't really care about you."

Dahar didn't reply right away. Ayman let him think about what he had said to him. After a few minutes, Ayman said, "Samir, let me help you. With the right information, we can possibly get the authorities to release you and allow you to go back to St. Maarten."

"You can do that? What kind of information do you need?"

"You were sent here on a mission by the Brotherhood against the Americans - true?"

"I can't talk about that. I took an oath. I can't betray my comrades."

"You don't have to talk about your comrades, just yourself."

"Well, what would I need to tell the Americans?"

"If you just relate to them what you were instructed to do here in America, that might be enough for them to release you. The Federal authorities could then perhaps talk with the judge about these assault charges, too."

"I don't know, Mr. Ayman. This is very confusing for me."

"Listen, Samir, you have a choice. If there is an attack here, you could go to jail forever. Tell the authorities about your instructions, and you can go free: back to St. Maarten to your lady friend and the bakery shop."

"How much would I have to tell them?"

"Why don't we work this out together? You tell me the story, and then I'll help you put together the information that we think the Americans would accept?"

"Yes, but then my comrades would know I talked to the police. I can't do that. My family would disown me. I would be disgraced."

"No one would ever know you talked with the authorities. They have many sources and can announce that the information came from some foreign country, perhaps a friendly intelligence service. They do this all the time to protect people."

"Yes, but you said I would have to go before a judge for the fight. What would I say there?"

"The authorities can work out a scenario with the judge. You may even have to spend a month in jail here, but then you would be free, and no one would ever know you talked with the authorities." Ayman could tell from the questions posed by Dahar that he really did want to get out of this mess and go back to St. Maarten. He was coming around slowly as Ayman was able to counter his objections.

Dahar sat in silence for a few minutes and then asked, "What would I say to the Brotherhood?"

"You could tell them that this other man started a fight with you and you fought back, fearing for your life. The cops put you in jail, and you couldn't go on your mission. That is the truth."

"Yes, but what if they want me to come back here on another mission? "

"You tell them that you have done your part for the cause and now want to get on with your life."

"Yes, but I took an oath to die for Allah. I failed him and the Brotherhood."

"Tell them this experience has changed you. You now want to be a holy man and recruit others to the Muslim faith. I don't think they will waste their time bothering you in St. Maarten."

"But I never studied the Koran or went to college. How can I be a holy man?"

"Talk with your lady friend. You said she is very knowledgeable about many religions. Let her teach you. It's not like you have to become an Imam. You can buy the bakery and be known in the community as a very religious Muslim. We all don't have to be Jihadists to serve Allah."

Dahar digested Ayman's words and seemed to be coming to a decision. After a while, he said, "Okay, Mr. Ayman, let us work out what we say to the Americans, and then I'll make a decision."

"Good, that is a fair way to arrive at the correct decision. You tell me the story from start to finish, and then we will work out what to say to them."

Dahar proceeded to explain how he was contacted by the Brotherhood, and then the instructions and details of what he was to do once he came to America. Ayman did not interrupt and allowed Dahar to complete his story, including what happened in the bar on Friday. When he had finished, Ayman thought for a minute before asking a few crucial questions.

"So all you know so far is you were to drive a car and be a martyr for Allah, but you don't know where or when this is to occur."

"No, Mr. Ayman. They are very security conscious. I just knew I was to come here with others, that someone would contact us and then give us our instructions."

"Yes, but what happened to the cars you brought up here from New Jersey?"

"Oh, two of my comrades were contacted and told to deliver the cars to someone here last Friday. I don't know any details, and I never saw anyone to talk about that after the fight in the bar. I assume the cars were taken to a safe place here for them to be prepared with explosives."

"Samir, you will need to tell the Americans everything you told me. You are not betraying your comrades, because you don't know when or where these explosions will occur."

"Yes, but I can't give them the names of my brothers."

"You certainly can, because I am sure the police went to your hotel after your arrest and spoke with the manager there. All your names are listed in the hotel records."

"I never thought about that," said Dahar.

"All right, here is what we do. You go back to your cell and don't talk to anyone. I will contact a source in Homeland Security and tell him we can provide some information, but they have to promise to help you."

"Who is Homeland Security?"

"They are the same type of agency as the FBI. They work with the FBI on terrorist things. My source will work with the FBI and the police here to assist you. They will probably want to talk with you to get more details. Just be truthful with them, and things will work out okay."

"I don't know what else I can say. I don't know any more information."

"Dahar, you told me everything, didn't you? If they find you lying to them, they will lock you up forever."

"Mr. Ayman. I swear on your Koran, I am telling you everything!"

"All right, Samir Dahar, I believe you, and I will be back to you very soon."

Ayman called the guard, and he took Dahar back to his jail cell.

CHAPTER FORTY-TWO

Unbeknownst to Dahar, the entire conversation with Ayman Siede was broadcast and recorded in a room down the hall from the interview room. A French-speaking police officer provided a simultaneous summary of what Dahar was telling Siede. In addition, they had a secure telephone link to DHS Headquarters, where Scott Hartley and several of the senior staff were also listening to the conversation.

Patrick and John were in the police station interview room, along with Chief Daniels, Captain Dan Bowman from the Maine State Police, and Sheriff Roger Tate. When Ayman Siede came in after the interview, he was given a standing ovation for his performance. While they still didn't know what they needed to stop an attack, they now knew there was, in fact, to be an attack, and that cars were being fitted with explosives somewhere in southern Maine.

Ayman Siede stated he believed that Dahar had told him everything he knew about the attack. "Dahar seems to have become conflicted over his role as a Jihadist and his desire to continue his life in St. Maarten," said Ayman. "He obviously has had time while in jail here to consider all these things. I think our conversation eventually brought him around to expressing what he really desires: a pleasant life in St. Maarten." Ayman also believed that the sophisticated operational security procedures employed by this unknown group indicated a well-planned operation.

John mentioned that the two males they had surveilled from Burlington ended up in Portland, too. "Given those two guys and the three others who came here with Dahar, we could be looking at five or six cars with explosives," said Patrick.

"If that's true," said Hartley, "we are not just looking at targets in Maine. They could be targeting anywhere along the East Coast. With the 4th of July holiday this week, they will have numerous events with large crowds to target, especially in the major cities."

"If that's the case, why would they have come to Maine?" asked Chief Daniels.

"Perhaps they believed it would be safer to gather the cars, explosives, and people in the countryside, and then dispatch them to their targets," said Patrick.

"That's a good point," said Hartley. "Law enforcement has broken up a lot of the planned attacks that were started in the larger cities. They may have concluded it is too easy to be compromised by informants, so they decided to move to the country."

"Yes, but that begs the question as to where they would go here," said Daniels. "If they have no presence here, how would they find a place to rent and set up operation here without arousing suspicion by the local residents?"

"I agree," said Patrick, "unless they were able to rent a large estate or farm here and bring everything they need with them."

"They could have co-opted someone who has a place up here, or even have a local sympathizer who is a face to the community," said John.

"As you know," said Sheriff Tate, "Maine is a vacationland, and we are now in our busiest season. People from all over the world come here in the summer, and no one pays much attention to them."

"Yes, and the Portland area has a very diverse population compared to other locations in Maine," said Captain Bowman. "I agree with Sheriff Tate, they could be here among us, and, as long as they were careful, no one would have any suspicion about them."

"Well, that complicates our problem," said Hartley. "If we agree that Maine is a preparation area, then how do we get the public to assist us without causing a panic? Several of my senior staff have been passing me notes while we are speaking, recommending we have a press conference in Portland."

"Okay," said Daniels, "but what can we say? If we broadcast our theory about Maine being the preparation location, then what do the authorities do in Boston and the other large cities on the East Coast? Cancel all the public festivities?"

"I know," said Hartley. "We don't have any good choices. But if attacks occur and we did nothing, how could we live with ourselves?"

"Maybe it's time to be just honest with our people and tell them what we know and what we don't know," said Patrick. "This kind of problem has been coming for a long time, and now we have to face it."

"Yes, but we can't have citizens attacking every Muslim and mosque in the country because they think they are terrorists," said Hartley.

"No, but we have become so PC we are afraid to be honest with the public," said John. "We didn't start this terrorist war, and either we fight and save lives, or we surrender."

"If they are still here, they don't have many roads to take them out of Maine," said Bowman. "The Maine Turnpike is the only major road south, and, if we could get some good intelligence, we could stop them before they got out of the state. For example, we could screen cars at the York Toll Plaza before letting them move on south to New Hampshire. Given that these people are not from here, they probably would stick to the main roads."

"Well, that is a possibility," said Hartley. "Look, why don't you guys brainstorm all the various options, while I call Deputy Director Wolsey, and we'll fly up this afternoon. We have secure communications on the plane, so Wolsey can talk with his federal counterparts here and let them know what we've got. We also need to get a few governors into the loop. Wolsey knows all the political heads he needs to brief, and the rest of us will work on options for the decision-makers. Does that look like a preliminary plan to you guys?"

"All the heads are nodding YES here," said Patrick. "So we will see you in a few hours."

"Let us know your ETA, and I'll have a car pick you up at the airport," said Daniels.

"Okay, and I'll be talking to you from the plane," said Hartley.

CHAPTER FORTY-THREE

Deputy Director William Wolsey and his operations officer, Scott Hartley, were airborne to Portland, Maine, within two hours. Scott had briefed Wolsey in the car on their way to Andrews Air Force Base, and Wolsey began calling his counterparts at FBI, CIA, and the White House Situation Room, and others who could assist them. The Director of DHS, Margaret Bollino, had returned from her European meetings but now was on a one-week camping trip in the wilds of Oregon, and Wolsey was unable to raise her on the phone.

"Remind me next week, Scott, that we have to get a SATPHONE for the Director when she goes off on these camping trips. She is undoubtedly out of cell phone range and won't be able to join in until after this situation is over."

Scott nodded yes, but privately thought it was for the best that the Director was out of touch. She was great at schmoozing with the politicos, especially those who could move her career along, but wouldn't be of any operational help to them. "Has anyone you've talked to come up with a better idea than a press conference to get the public aware and asking for their assistance?"

"No, as long as we do it. I tend to think that, if this alert backfires and we cause a panic, the other agencies will pretend they had 'hands off', and we will take the hit. The White House doesn't want any of this to stick to the President so he can say he wasn't aware of what DHS was going to do, and then he can fire all of us. This is a bucket of shit, and none of these folks want to be near it."

"What about the FBI, they could take over if they wanted to?"

"They have pledged any assistance we need, but graciously said we should continue as lead agency, since we have all the background information."

"Right! One consolation is we get to call the shots, and we don't have some politician telling us to do something stupid. If we're going to screw up, I would rather have it be because of something we did, rather than orders from some publicity-seeking politician."

"Agreed, Scott, but, if this goes well, we will have a cast of others proclaiming we did what they told us to do. Nothing changes in Washington, DC; everything is political."

They worked on some draft comments for Wolsey to use at the press conference. Hartley called Daniels and asked him to have his public affairs officer notify the media, and the subject would be on possible terrorist attacks. They discussed who should be on the dais with Wolsey and the time for the conference. It was agreed, since it was a Sunday evening, that it would be best to hold it after dark, when most people would be home.

When Wolsey came onto the stage at Portland's City Hall, there were chiefs and heads of local, state, and local federal agencies, the mayor of Portland, and the Maine Emergency Management Chief representing the Governor's office. Chief Daniels introduced all the members on the dais and then introduced William Wolsey.

Good Evening. I have a short statement to read, and then I will entertain a few questions. Please understand that there are questions I cannot answer, due to the methods and sources that have alerted us to the present situation. I also don't want to panic the public, but we believe we have a duty to tell you what we know and that we need the public's help if anyone has information to assist us in resolving our situation.

Recently, we received credible information from foreign intelligence sources that an unknown terrorist group planned an attack against the United States. In cooperation with many of the agencies represented on this stage, agents of the Department of Homeland Security have gathered information that leads us to conclude that an attempted attack is real. However, we don't yet know where or when, but we believe the attack or attacks will occur in conjunction with our 4th of July holiday celebrations this coming week.

What we do believe is that there will be attempted car bomb attacks. We believe that five to six cars have been brought to Southern Maine for preparation and then will be dispatched to sites on the East Coast for attack. We don't yet know the name of this alleged terrorist group or the names of the people involved.

We are asking the public, if you have any information that could help us in any way to prevent these attacks, that you call the 1-800 number listed on the bottom of your TV screen. We want to emphasize that no one should take any action against any persons, organizations, or property. If you have information, call us. If you don't have any information, do not engage in any action that will cause you to be arrested and prosecuted.

We are currently searching US Customs data systems to identify any foreign individuals who have recently entered the United States and have overstayed their visa or travelled to an area of the United States other than what they stated upon entering the country. We already have the names of six individuals who have been identified and whose names and photographs appear on this chart. Again, I want to emphasize that, at this time, these people have only overstayed their visit, and we want to find them and clear them from our investigation. If they are watching this evening, I ask them to come forward and notify the nearest police agency. Other names will be forthcoming.

I will take a few questions.

Local TV news anchor: Are you asking cities and towns to cancel their 4th of July celebrations?

No. We believe each community best understands their security preparations and capabilities and that they should make that decision.

AP Wire reporter: Do you know anything about these cars, or what type of person would be driving them?

Not yet. We are looking at a couple of possible vehicles and will announce that information as it comes to us. We also can't rule out that the recruited drivers are all foreigners.

Local newspaper reporter: How do you know that these attacks won't be carried out in Maine?

We don't know that information. However, we believe, if there are five or six vehicles involved, that the planners of these attacks would also send them to places other than Maine.

Local TV newscaster: It seems like you don't know very much information, so why should we believe your estimate that these attacks will take place?

As I stated at the beginning of my remarks, there is some sensitive information that I can't release that leads us to the assessment that planned attacks are real. If we knew where the perpetrators are located, we would go get them. We have a duty to protect our citizens. We also have a duty to warn them, even when we don't have all the information. I'll take one more question.

Local newspaper reporter: *Sources tell me that the Portland police arrested a foreigner Friday evening who was involved in a bar fight. Are you looking at him?*

We are looking for terrorists, not people who get into bar fights. Chief Daniels told my agents that they did arrest a foreigner Friday evening, and he has refused to talk with them. We doubt that any person involved in these attacks would be in any bar and especially get into an altercation and be arrested.

Again, if anyone has any information, please notify your local police department or us. Our agents are trained to assess people, and that is why we don't want the public taking any action on their own. As we get more information we will provide it to the public. Thank you.

Director Wolsey and the other officials on the dais departed the stage and entered a room that had been secured by the police. "Well, what is your assessment of how it went?" asked Wolsey.

"I am glad we discussed an answer about the foreigner we arrested," said Chief Daniels. "As much as we have compartmentalized the information, the local media has good sources in our department."

"Given all the people who were present when the police broke up the bar fight, it is not surprising that the media got some information," said John Carver.

The assessment of the group was that, for the most part, the media seemed to be positive and helpful, and that all the press releases highlighted that the public should take no action on their own. Two of the local TV stations planned to do *"man in the street"* polling on Monday, so there would be public feedback to Wolsey's comments.

They discussed how the various agencies involved would respond to calls that would come in as a result of the press conference. All in the room knew that most all of the reports would lead nowhere, but they had to respond to them. An operations room was set up in the Portland police headquarters with representatives from all the agencies. Sheriff Tate and Chief Daniels were going to send officers to all the vacation rental property firms in the morning to identify people renting large estates or farms in the area. They would ask local law enforcement in surrounding areas in Southern Maine to also conduct these leads. The Maine State Police volunteered to dispatch officers to the York Toll Plaza on the Maine Turnpike in the morning and begin screening cars heading south to New Hampshire. It would slow traffic considerably, but most of the heavy traffic was coming north into Maine for the 4th of July holiday.

Having no more to do at the present time, Wolsey thanked everyone and requested they meet again Monday afternoon at 5:00 to assess the situation.

CHAPTER FORTY-FOUR

Ben and Aarif had been alerted to the press conference by Destiny, and they watched it in the living room of the main house. Destiny chose to watch it on a TV in her bedroom. She was fuming that all of this mess could possibly involve her and ruin her law career. She went back downstairs when the press conference ended. Aarif was pacing the living room and muttering something in a strange language.

"Well, I see you geniuses have managed to make the big time," she said. "We now have every cop in Southern Maine looking for us, including the Feds."

"Be still," said Aarif. "You don't know your place."

"Don't shush me, you foreign ingrate. I don't know why I ever agreed to this nonsense. Ben, I want you, Josef or Aarif or whatever the hell your name is, and all these other wackos out of here by the morning. Don't you realize the cops will now be checking all the places in the county, especially places that have barns? So, out you go, and take everyone and everything with you. I don't want a speck of evidence that others were here for when the cops show up."

"We were just talking about leaving early in the morning," shouted Ben. "So you don't have to yell and start bossing us around. You agreed to this, you know. So don't get so uppity when we have a problem."

"I didn't agree to what you have done, bringing all these strange people here, disrupting my summer vacation, and now possibly getting involved with the police. You and your buddy here are the problem, and I don't think you told me the truth about what you are going to do. You never said we would have all these foreigners running around here with beads and prayers rugs and muttering in a strange language. I don't want to know anything except you came and now you all are out of here in the morning!" she shouted.

Destiny stormed out of the room. Aarif, who obviously had never been the recipient of a woman's wrath, finally regained his composure. "Ben, she is crazy. No woman should talk to us like that. Have you talked to Ghanem? Has he agreed to take care of her?"

"Yes, Aarif. He will stay behind and take care of things. I was surprised he didn't ask for more money. She will get what is coming to her."

"Perhaps he didn't ask for money because he is dreaming of playing with her before he finishes his work." Aarif chuckled at his own words.

"We have a lot of work to do before we get out of here in the morning," said Ben. "She is correct that the cops will probably come around all these farms, so we have to be sure everything that could point to our presence is taken away."

"What do we do with the extra stuff?"

"We clean everything out and put it in the cars, even the food. Why don't you get the men working on that now while I copy maps for every driver. The sun comes up about 6:00, and I want all of us to be ready to leave then."

"Did you talk with Ghanem about rigging the car for Washington, DC, to go off on July 4th? That was to be the car for Dahar. The Hussein brothers agreed to drive the car down there and park it on the mall. They are not martyrs, so they will drop the car and take a plane towards home."

"Yes, Aarif, I did. I also told him to load the 9mm automatics and put them in the cars, too."

"Ben, I can't believe that Dahar turned on us and talked with the police. I heard that police chief say Dahar wouldn't talk to them, but he must have been their source. Maybe they drugged him. What do you think?"

"I don't think he is the informant. All he knew was to come to the States and someone would meet him. He sure didn't know about our two drivers who came here from Canada. Their photos were on that board the DHS guy showed on TV. So it must have been someone higher up who informed on us."

"Ben, the only person at our Mosque who knew the details of our operation is Sheikh Al Sakhr, and he would not talk with anyone."

"Then it must be someone back in the Middle East who helped with the operation - someone who knew about the drivers and how they got here."

"Do you think the Americans know about our targets?"

"I don't think so. Those guys overseas just knew we needed drivers and we were going to hit multiple targets. They didn't know the targets or the dates."

"This always is our downfall, Ben. The infidels throw money at our people, and the weak ones betray us. It is our curse."

"It will be okay, Aarif. We get our cars out of Maine, and we will be okay."

"Alright, I will get the men moving so we can get some sleep. They have a long day ahead of them. We all will say morning prayers together before we set out on our journey in the morning."

Ben had been studying a Maine map and thought the police would focus on the interstate highways. Certainly, they would try to spot the cars and drivers when they went through the tolls on the Maine Turnpike. Therefore, he wanted another route out of Maine. There weren't many choices driving south. He decided to route the drivers into Portland, and over to South Portland. From there, they would travel on Route 1 into New Hampshire. They would follow Route 1 south until they got past the Hampton Tolls and then proceed onto I-95 and on to their destinations. This route would take more time and be congested in many of the towns along the way, but he believed this would help hide the cars and drivers as they escaped south. He then marked out routes for each driver to get them to their destination. Fortunately, he had been able to get maps of every state and city he needed at the Delorme map store just south of Freeport on I-295.

He also marked out the route that he and Aarif would take to leave Maine. They had decided to head west to Burlington, Vermont, and cross the border into Canada. He had made reservations at a hotel in Montreal. Their plan was to stay there a few days until they could assess how their attacks had gone, and then decide how and when to come back into the United States, if at all. Aarif had plenty of money, so they could travel outside the United States until things had quieted down. Finished his work, he headed into the den and to sleep on the couch. He would get his things in the morning from the bedroom he had shared with Destiny. Hopefully, she would quiet down while they prepared to leave the property.

CHAPTER FORTY-FIVE

Sunrise came early. Aarif led the group in morning prayers. Ben then gave a pep talk, telling them they were Jihadist warriors ready to strike again at the Infidels, just like their brothers had done on 9/11. He passed out their maps and money and again emphasized they were to reach their destinations in time for the American holiday on July 4th. Only if the police cornered them should they set off their explosives prematurely. None of them were aware that authorities were looking for them.

After a quick breakfast, they proceeded to their cars. Rabiah Abdou and Nasheed had prepared food for their journey, and each driver had bottles of water. They drove down close to the highway and waited for a signal from Ben to drive out onto the highway and go on their way. Ben was staggering the cars at 15-minute intervals so they wouldn't be bunched up together. They were late getting off, but fortunately the morning traffic had picked up as people headed for work. This would help them blend in with the traffic. Ben managed to get all four cars onto the highway without them being spotted coming out of the farm.

They originally had wanted to hit six targets, but Ghanem had refused to drive a car. Ben and Aarif certainly would not take part, but they did decide to drive the extra car to the parking area at the Maine Mall on the way out of town this morning. The mall was near the airport, and they had to drop Nasheed there so she could catch a flight back to New Jersey. Ben had Ghanem rig the car with explosives to go off later that day. He wanted to send a signal to the police that Maine was not just a preparation locale for the attacks. He hoped the explosion would create panic and some confusion for the police in Maine. The other four targets would create widespread panic and cause great destruction. They had finally settled on the 4th of July celebrations in Boston, New York, Philadelphia, and Washington, DC. The drivers would be getting to their targets early but had been instructed to find a motel near the target site until it was time to activate. Photographs of each of the target sites had been provided them, along with possible routes to each site.

Ben drove back up to the house and went inside to get his things. Aarif walked through all the rooms and the barn to make sure nothing had been left behind. He met Ghanem in the barn and told him to carry out his part as soon as Ben and he left the farm. Ghanem gave him a high five and told Aarif he was looking forward to a very busy morning. Aarif smiled at him but inwardly thought Ghanem was not a real Muslim warrior. He viewed him as an opportunist who was taking advantage of them. However, he hoped that Ghanem would torture Destiny before he killed her. She was poison and deserved to die.

Destiny had been watching from the bedroom as Ben had driven up to the house. When Ben entered the bedroom, he was surprised to see his clothes had been packed. "You can just leave, I have all your stuff in the suitcase. When you get back to California, you can also get your stuff out of my apartment. I have had it with you and that idiot friend of yours. You can go find a new patsy."

"We are going now," said Ben. "I assume you won't tell anyone about our adventure here."

"What, and get myself in trouble! I am staying here and seeing my friends. I'll say you had to go back early. I found that staying together these past weeks convinced me that I need to look further for a mate, so it was convenient for you to leave now."

"I guess that will do it," said Ben. Neither said goodbye. He picked up his suitcase and went down the stairs and out to where the cars were parked. Aarif was there with Nasheed. He would not allow her to go inside to say farewell to Destiny. They decided that Aarif would drive the Toyota and Nasheed ride with him. They would follow Ben, driving the car with explosives to the Maine Mall parking area, where he would leave the car. They would then drive Nasheed to the airport and continue on their way west to Canada.

Destiny was eating breakfast when Ghanem walked into the house. "What the…"

"Don't get upset, Destiny, I'm leaving, too. I just didn't want to go with them."

"Well, how are you going to leave? Didn't they take all the cars?"

"Yes, but you need to listen to what I say. It is important for your safety."

"Why should I be concerned with my safety? This is my place, and I haven't done anything wrong."

"Just listen, Destiny. Let me finish what I need to say."

"Okay. Go ahead, I'm listening."

"Destiny, Ben and Aarif want me to kill you and blow up this place."

"What are you saying?" she yelled at him.
"Just calm down and listen to me, okay? You don't see me doing anything to you, so let me finish."

273

"All right, but no bullshit. Tell me what is going on."

"I am telling the truth. They want me to kill you and blow up the house. I told them I would do it so they would leave things to me. I have no plan to kill you or blow up anything."

"Well, what do you want?"

"I have a plan, and you need to help me with it."

"What kind of plan?"

"Just listen, and then we can talk. They don't trust you, especially Aarif. He wants you dead. You don't like him."

"I hate him, I hate them both. They could ruin my life with their stupid operation."

"I know, I know. I don't like Aarif either. He looks down on me because I am a Black Muslim. He thinks we are inferior to him and was just using me. Those guys are going to blow up a lot of people, including my black brothers. I think we can stop them."

"Yes, but then they will involve me."

"Listen to my plan, and I think you will be okay."

"They are gone. How can we stop them?"

""Listen to this. I put you down in the basement cellar. I get away in your car. In less than an hour, I am at the airport. I call 911 and tell them the terrorists were at your farm. They have locked you in the basement of the house. When the cops come, you will have a list of the license plates and description of the cars, to give to the police."

"Yes, but why didn't the terrorists kill me or something?"

"Easy, one of the terrorists turns out to be Ben. You never knew that until all these guys show up and they take you prisoner. They left this black guy here to kill you and blow up the house, but he put you in the cellar and told you he would call 911 when he got to the airport. He also gave you the list of the cars and licenses."

"Yes, but how does that help you with the cops?"

"Well, we never used names around you, and I didn't kill you or blow up the house."

"Yes, but they will show me photos. Weren't you in jail last year or so?"

"Yeah, but you know, all us black guys look alike and you only saw me once or twice." He laughed as he said that, and she laughed, too.

"I don't think that look-alike stuff will fool the cops. I'll tell them you changed your mind when you found out what they were going to do."

"Okay, that sounds better. Look, we don't have a lot of time. If you can think up a better story while you're in the cellar, have at it. You are the law lady and have a way with words."

"Ghanem, they really wanted you to kill me and blow up this place? I can believe that of Aarif, but I thought Ben was the man who wanted to marry me."

"I know. It's hard to believe. Come on, we got to move."

Ghanem gave her the list of the cars and license plate numbers. She grabbed a book to read in the basement and also gave him the keys to the farm's vehicle and her cell phone. He told her he would leave the phone in the car at the airport.

He opened the floor entrance to the cellar. Destiny gave him a hug and went down into the basement. "Hurry," she said. "I don't want to spend long down here, and we need the cops to find these guys."

"I'll be quick. Just remember, you have to convince the cops you were a prisoner. It's the only way to save yourself."

"Don't worry. All I have to do is think of that rat Aarif, and I'll be the cops' star witness."

CHAPTER FORTY-SIX

Ghanem pulled into the short-term section of the Portland Jetport parking garage. He dialed 911 and told the operator the police needed to hurry out to the Carter farm near Paine's Corner, because the terrorists had been there and Destiny Carter was locked in the basement. He also said there was a list of the vehicles and state license numbers of the vehicles they were going to use for the bombings. He hung up, and locked the car with the keys and cell phone in the car.

Taking his suitcase, he went out of the garage, crossed over to the baggage arrival area, and hailed a taxi. "I want to go to the Concord bus station in town," he told the driver.

"You're flying and now going to take a bus," said the driver.

"Yeah, I'm going up to Bangor, to see relatives, and it's cheaper to take the bus from here than to fly up there."

"I hear you," said the driver. "You're not the first customer I've driven to the bus station. "

When Ghanem entered the Concord Coach Lines terminal, he purchased a one-way ticket to Logan Airport in Boston. He had to show an ID to purchase the ticket and tell the clerk what airline he would be flying in order to check his suitcase on the bus. "You are all set, Mr. Smith," the clerk said, "Enjoy your flight. Is this a vacation trip?"

"Well, I was on vacation up here, but now I have to get back to work," said Ghanem.

"Where is home?" asked the clerk.

"I am heading back to Utah," he said.

"Oh, I was out there last year skiing. That's a cool place. Well, have a safe trip," said the clerk. "Your bus is leaving in twenty minutes, and the line is at the B door to my right." The line for tickets was getting longer, so Ghanem had to move on.

Approximately 3 hours later, the bus pulled into Logan Airport, and Ghanem got off at the Delta terminal. When the bus pulled away, he stayed outside and waited for an airport shuttle bus that drove passengers to the other terminals. He took the bus to the American Airlines terminal and went up to the counter to check in. He had to show his U.S. passport, since his final destination was Aruba. Ghanem was now traveling as Charles Saunders.

"You will have a 2-hour layover in Miami," said the ticket agent, "but the flight to Aruba is showing on schedule. Your gate here is Number 22 off to the left side from here, where you go through security. Is this a vacation or business, Mr. Saunders?"

"Unfortunately, I have to work when I get there, but I'll manage to get to the beach."

"Well, enjoy, and have a good flight, Mr. Saunders."

✍

Melissa Tate, the daughter of Sheriff Tate, was working the day shift at the Central 911 Dispatch office and had taken the call from Ghanem. She tried to get more information from him, but he hung up after giving his information. She replayed the recording of the call, filling in information in the notes she had jotted down when he called. She had heard an airplane in the background while he was talking and wondered if the call came from the Jetport.

She called out to Deputy Bruce Aaron, who was working the Paine's Corner area. "Bruce, this is Melissa. What is your location?"

"I'm pulling into the store at Paine's. In fact, I was just getting ready to call you that I would be on break for ten minutes or so. I'm meeting Tom Longley for coffee. We need to exchange information on what places he's checked in this area this morning. Oh, here he is now."

"Well, I have another one for you to check. It's the Carter farm. Caller said the terrorists had been there and that they had put a woman in the basement. Probably another crank call, but the Sheriff said to check them all out."

"Hey, Melissa, this is Tom. Did you say the Carter farm?"

"Hi Tom. You're working double shifts today, too. Yes, the caller said the Carter farm. Do you know the place?"

"My wife's friend, Destiny Carter, and her boyfriend are here for a few weeks this summer. I haven't been over there, but they have been to our house for dinner. It's just down the road here. Bruce and I can run over and see if they are home."

"Okay, let me know what you find, so I can close this complaint out."

"Will do."

They drove to the farm in Tom's State Police car. The gate in the driveway was open, so they didn't buzz for entry, but drove right up to the house. They saw no signs of life and noticed the doors to the garage were open but no cars there. The large doors to one of the barns were open, too.

"Looks like no one is home," said Bruce. "I'll go rap on the door just in case." He walked up and both knocked and rang the bell. He waited a few minutes, but no one answered. He tried the knob, and the door opened. Before entering, he motioned to Tom, who left the car and joined him at the front door.

"Caller said a woman was locked in the basement, so I guess we have good cause to enter the house."

"Yes," said Tom. They entered, and Tom called out: "Destiny, it's Tom Longley and Deputy Bruce Aaron. Are you home?"

No response. "I wonder where the door to the basement is?" asked Bruce.

"I've never been here," said Tom. "Let's look around." As they came into the hall between the kitchen and the living room, they heard yelling from below.

"There is latch on the floor under that table," said Bruce.

They moved the table and pulled on the latch, and a door opened to the cellar below. There was a light on, and a face appeared. "Thank God, thank God you're here," cried Destiny. She bounded up the stairs and into Tom's arms. She was crying and hugging him and jabbering all at once.

"It's okay, Destiny. You're safe; no one is going to hurt you. Are you alone? Where is Ben?"

Bruce gave her some tissues from a box on the table. She was still sobbing but trying to answer Tom's questions. "He's...gone. He left with the others."

"What others?" asked Tom.

"These foreigners. They came here and took me prisoner. Ben was with them. I didn't know it. They just showed up and took over. None of them spoke to me, except this horrible man. He is called Aarif or Josef, but that may not be his real name. He is the leader. They wanted to kill me, but this black guy called Ghanem saved me after they left. Oh, Tom, this is horrible." She was still trembling and started crying again.

Bruce keyed his mike and called dispatch. "Melissa, there may be something to this call. We found Destiny Carter locked in the basement and her boyfriend gone. She says there were foreigners here. Alert the Sheriff, and also we need a medic to look at Destiny. "

"Okay, and I'll alert the Operations Center in Portland, since they are controlling the search. Bruce, the caller said there was a list of cars and license plates. Can you ask her if she knows about that?"

"Sure. Destiny, is there a list of the cars these people were driving?"

She nodded her head and pointed to the kitchen but continued sobbing. Bruce went into the kitchen and saw a list on the table. It was exactly as the caller had told Melissa.

"I found it, Melissa. And on the bottom there is a scribbled note that Destiny's car is at the Jetport."

"That makes sense. I thought I heard an airplane during the call. Look, read me the car descriptions and license plates, and I'll get a BOLO on the wire ASAP. Then all law enforcement in the area will be on the lookout for those cars. We need to intercept these guys."

Bruce read her the information and almost froze when he saw the last car. "Oh my God, the note under the last car says it has been parked in the Maine Mall parking lot and will go off around mid-day."

"I got that," said Melissa. "I am alerting the South Portland police, the Operations Center, and the bomb squad. Is there any other info I should know? I need to get all these alerts out now, and then I'll get back to you."

"No, just get all that out, and Tom and I will stand by here until help arrives. Oh, we will need an evidence collection team, too."

Tom guided Destiny to a couch in the living room. She sobbed quietly, and he just let her be so she could calm down. There would be time enough for all the questions once all the detectives and federal agents arrived.

Bruce conducted a walk-through of the house and the large annex. He found nothing of interest in his cursory inspection. He also went out to the garage and barns, just to be sure there was no one else on the property. He wondered how this day would end.

CHAPTER FORTY-SEVEN

Melissa's BOLO and a call to the Operations Center caused a massive movement by Law Enforcement. With license numbers and car descriptions, they could put out a general call in the media, asking the public to assist the police in sighting the vehicles. The alert also contained the warning to just call the police but not to approach any vehicle or individual. The question was, did the cars already get out of Maine, or were they hiding here? Law enforcement in neighboring states was also included in the alert.

Management at the Maine Mall was called and immediately locked down the building, until the police could find the car and the bomb squad defused the explosives. It was decided to move people into the main corridors of the mall, since there would be more protection if an explosion occurred in one of the parking lots. Police also manned all the entrances to the mall parking lots to stop people arriving to shop. The surrounding streets were closed, and adjacent businesses were evacuated as a precaution. Of course, this also triggered a gathering of the media and TV trucks, and reporters began live coverage of the event.

≪

Nasir Ahmed, one of the drivers who arrived from Vermont, was very jittery this morning and had not paid close attention to Ben's directions. He somehow took a few wrong turns and found himself lost in Portland. His rambling brought him down to the Old Port area and then up through the Munjoy Hill section of the city. He eventually found a sign pointing to I-295, and he remembered Ben had said they could get on that road to find Route 1 to New Hampshire.

Nasir failed to notice what direction he was headed when he accessed onto I-295. He didn't know the area at all, but there was a lot of traffic, so he assumed he was headed to New Hampshire. He was not an experienced driver and focused on the road immediately ahead of him, so he had little time to read the road signs. However, after 2 hours on the road, he was approaching a tollbooth. There was also a large sign for a rest area. He decided to take that exit and stop and see how much farther he had to drive to reach New Hampshire. After parking the car, he entered the building, used the bathroom, and purchased some snacks. He spotted a map of Maine on a wall with the major highways highlighted. Upon searching the map, he discovered from the "YOU ARE HERE" symbol that he had been headed in the wrong direction for the past 2 hours and needed to change direction. While this concerned him, he knew that he had plenty of time, since his target was in Boston.

∽

Scott Hartley was sitting, having a cup of coffee with Patrick and John Carver in the Operations Center at the Portland Police Station. Deputy Director Wolsey had gone back to Washington. They were looking over all the alert notices that had been sent out by the dispatch center. Another team sitting at an adjacent table was brainstorming leads that could possibly locate and neutralize the terrorists.

Chief Daniels came into the room and approached them. "I just got off the phone with the Chief of the South Portland Police, who is at the Maine Mall. He said the bomb squad has neutralized the explosives, and they are moving the car by truck to a remote site for evidence processing. The ATF is also there assisting. The most interesting development was that there was no detonator for the explosives."

"But that is bomb making 101," said John.

"I know, unless this car was rigged at the last minute and they overlooked a detonator."

"Have the police made that fact known to the press?" asked Hartley.

"No, and we talked about keeping it quiet. I told the Chief I would talk to you about it and get back to him."

"I think we should say nothing about that," said Patrick. "The bad guys are expecting an explosion at the Maine Mall. When that doesn't occur, it could put some psychological pressure on them."

"I agree," said Scott. "Anything that tends to disrupt their plans will cause them to question their operational security and planning, let alone do they have a traitor in their midst."

"Well, it looks like we're all in agreement," said Daniels. "I'll call the Chief back and tell him that. By the way, dispatch tells me that nothing has come back on the agency traces on this guy Ghanem."

"If we can get a good photo from either the airport or the bus station, we can circulate it to the media," said John.

"I think that is our best lead right now," said Hartley. "Ghanem sounds like a foreign nickname that never got associated with a real person in our federal agency files. By the way, has anything new come from the interview of the Carter woman?"

"Nothing that helps us right now."

"We will get a briefing later today by our DHS agents that are with her out at her farm," said Hartley.

❦

Nasir Ahmed headed south on the Maine Turnpike. The traffic was heavy, and Nasir hadn't seen any police cars all morning. Despite what Ben had said, he believed he was safe driving on this road, because he blended in with the rest of the cars. He also wasn't sure how to get over to this Route 1 road that Ben had mentioned. As he approached the Kennebunk service area some 2 hours later, he decided to stop again because he needed a bathroom. The main building was crowded with tourists, and no one paid any attention to him.

State Policeman Ron Tupper was sitting at the exit to the Kennebunk service area in an unmarked police vehicle, when he saw a red Honda Accord sedan with Massachusetts license plates go past him out onto the Turnpike. He didn't get all the numbers of the license, but enough to follow the car onto the main road. After he determined it was one of the wanted cars, he reduced speed and pulled into the slow lane. "Dispatch, this is Tupper out on the Turnpike heading south. I just left the Kennebunk service area and am following one of the wanted cars with Massachusetts's license plates. I am unmarked, so I can stay with him while you alert the cars at the York Toll Plaza."

"Roger that, Officer Tupper. I am alerting Lt. Goss, who is heading the detail at York. He will contact you for further instructions."

"Ron, this is Lt. Goss. I have Al Corbet and Judd Compton on the line with me. About 5 miles down the road, you will meet their two marked vehicles. The three of you are to fill all three lanes and set up a rolling roadblock, staying far enough back from the Subject. I want as few cars as possible coming into the toll plaza area when Subject arrives. We plan to let him come through the plaza and then block him about

500 yards away. I want to keep the cars behind you from coming through the tolls, so we have officers here to stop them once you get into the plaza area."

"Do you want us to be part of the blocking action past the tolls?" asked Compton.

"No, we have enough cars, a SWAT team, and the bomb guys here. Do come through the tolls as backup, in case we need to stop any cars that get past the officers in the toll stations. Once we stop him, hopefully we can take him without setting off an explosion. If there are no questions, just keep me posted on your ETA here. Ron, since you have the unmarked vehicle, I'll make you lead, in case we need to have you to move closer to Subject before the tolls. I am contacting our chopper, and they will join you from above as you move towards us here."

✍

Deputy Horace Cobb had been patrolling all morning and came into the town of Gorham, New Hampshire, to have lunch. He cruised slowly through Main Street and planned to stop at Marcy's restaurant, just west of the town on Route 2. As he pulled into the parking lot, he gazed at the vehicle license plates. There had been a major BOLO alert this morning because of possible terrorists in Maine, and one of the cars might be coming west to Canada. He almost pulled into a parking space when he saw a black Toyota Highlander with Florida plates parked along the side of the restaurant. He grabbed his clipboard and checked the plate number of the Toyota with his list. "My God," he said to himself. He grabbed his phone and yelled, "Dispatch, connect me with the sheriff!"

A few minutes later, Sheriff Hal Manner came on the line. "Horace, what's the problem?"

"You are not going to believe this, Sheriff, but I think we have one of those Maine terrorists right here in town."

"What do you mean?"

"I am looking at a Toyota with Florida plates, and the number matches the one on the BOLO list."

"Where are you?"

"I'm in the parking lot of Marcy's."

"Are you sure?"

"The make, model, color, and license plates match."

"Is anyone in the vehicle?"

"No, they must be in the restaurant."

"Okay, get out of the parking lot and set up surveillance where they can't see you when they come out. I'll round up some help from Gorham and the State cars that are in the area and get back to you. Keep me posted."

"Okay, Sheriff, I'm moving now."

CHAPTER FORTY-EIGHT

The news of the sighting of one of the terrorist vehicles on the Maine Turnpike flashed back to the Operations Center at the Portland Police Department. Captain Bowman briefed the group on how the Maine State Police were deployed at the York Toll Plaza and the plan to intercept the vehicle.

"This seems like a good plan to me," said Hartley. "I don't know what else we can do, even if we end up taking the driver out. Hopefully, we can avoid an explosion, but, under the circumstances, we don't have any good options."

There was agreement by all, and, at this point, there was not much they could do but await the confrontation. While they were discussing the York plan, word came that a second terrorist vehicle had been spotted in Gorham, New Hampshire.

"Apparently, they spotted the car at a restaurant, and the sheriff is organizing a team to intercept the vehicle," said Chief Daniels. "They are going to set up west of the town on Route 2, since they believe the terrorists are heading towards Canada."

"Is this the vehicle with the two ringleaders of the group?" asked Patrick.

"Yes. The vehicle is a Toyota Highlander with Florida plates, and the list we got from the farm mentioned that these two guys were headed to Burlington, Vermont, or Canada," said the Chief.

"Hopefully, they can take them alive, since they aren't supposed to have explosives," said Hartley.

"But we have to assume they are armed, even though we don't know what types of firearms they carry," said Patrick.

"We said 'armed and dangerous' when we sent out the alarm," said Chief Daniels.

"I know a few of the local cops over that way," said Sheriff Tate. "A number of them are hunters and very good marksmen. They won't need a SWAT team to take down these terrorists."

Bowman said that a State Police helicopter had joined the surveillance and would be providing a direct video link as the Subject entered the toll plaza and the blocking action to apprehend him.

～

Nasir drove out of the Kennebunk service area and joined the throng of cars heading south. He kept his speed at a pace that kept him flowing along with about 15 other cars. He felt safe being in the center with the other cars. Thus, he didn't look in his rear mirrors often at all and was oblivious to the fact that the Maine State Police had formed a rolling road-block, preventing his cluster of cars to get any bigger as they moved along the Turnpike. Nasir saw a large sign alerting that the toll plaza was six miles ahead and the price of the toll. As the vehicles got closer to the toll plaza, he realized there were lanes for cash and others reserved for something called EZ Pass. He didn't know what that was, and decided to go into a cash lane. Most all the toll lanes were open, so he had no trouble pulling into one near the center of the plaza. He noticed the toll taker had a uniform and badge, but assumed that was normal for such a job.

He paid his fare and started out of the plaza. He didn't notice that his was the only car leaving the plaza, until he merged into the three lanes of the highway heading south to New Hampshire. He thought that strange and looked back in the rear view mirror. As he did so, he saw vehicles block the three lanes behind him. When he focused around, he suddenly saw that the roadway ahead was blocked, and he had no way to escape. The northbound lanes on the other side were also blocked, so he couldn't cut across the median to the other side. He slowed and then stopped the car. What to do?

Nasir realized he was trapped. He slowly drove the car forward towards the roadblock of cars and trucks. "I can't get out of here," he thought, "but I can take all these cops down with me." He pressed the plunger to create the explosion. Ben had said it was on a timer and had an eight- to ten-minute delay. He couldn't reach his explosive vest, which was on the floor in the back seat, but, if he could hold off the cops until the delay expired, he could take them out when the car exploded.

"You, in the car," the voice came from a loudspeaker behind the barricade. "Stop the car, turn off the engine, and slowly get out of the car. Stop the car or we shoot out the tires."

Nasir continued forward a little and swung the car around so the trunk was now facing the barricade, and stopped. He estimated he was close enough for the blast to reach them, since the explosives were in the trunk. He decided to stay in the car and play for time.

The voice again ordered him to get out of the car, but Nasir ignored him.

The SWAT team leader told Lt. Goss they had a clear shot at the driver.

"Leave him be for now," said Goss. "Let's see if we can take him alive. We have lots of time. But if he gets out and starts shooting, you are clear to take him down. Don't shoot into the trunk area. It probably is where the explosives are, and we don't want to set them off."

The officials in the Operations Center watched the action from the helicopter feed. "I think Lt. Goss is right," said Patrick. "We have lots of time, and it would be nice to get him alive."

"Agree," Said Hartley. "We need to avoid the explosion, too, since we don't know how wide the path of it would be. That car is close with its trunk pointed towards the barricade. I assume the device is in there. We don't want to endanger any of our people."

"We just got a preliminary report on the explosive device from the vehicle at the Maine Mall," said Chief Daniels. "The device was in a plastic jug and is believed to contain a combination of urea-based fertilizer, ammonium nitrate, and nitric acid, which, with a few other materials, makes urea nitrate."

"That's the same stuff that was used in the 1993 World Trade Center bombing," said John Carver. "What about the detonator?"

"They found cordage, a timing mechanism, but no detonating charge," said Daniels.

"That is very strange," said Hartley. "One could almost think this is deliberate. That's why it would be great to get the device in this car without setting it off. But we can't take chances with our people so close to the vehicle."

"Actually," said Captain Bowman, "Lt. Goss has moved all his people back an extra 100 yards, and he and the SWAT team are prone on top of a trailer truck. We can see it now on the feed from the helicopter. He's telling me they have a good line of sight on the driver from there and can still take him out if he gets dangerous."

"Well, that makes me feel a little better," said Hartley. "Let's talk about what we do if this guy continues to sit in the car. Should we try to negotiate with him?"

"In what language?" asked Patrick.

"Yeah, I know, but let's assume this guy understands English. How about we fly a negotiator down there and see if we can get him to talk."

"Goss has a trained negotiator with him," said Bowman. "I'll tell him to see if he can get the Subject to talk."

⤚

In Gorham, New Hampshire, Sheriff Manner reported he was able to quickly gather enough law enforcement officers to set up a barricade west of the city on Route 2.

CHAPTER FORTY-NINE

Aarif and Ben had stopped at Marcy's restaurant for lunch in Gorham, New Hampshire, thinking they were safe from police surveillance. They had not been listening to the car radio and were unaware that police were looking for all of them. They entered the restaurant and chose a booth near the rear of the room, away from the kitchen and counter seats. After ordering from the menu, Ben left the table for the bathroom. On his return to the table, he passed the counter area and happened to glance at the TV on the wall. He was shocked at what he saw. An announcer was giving car descriptions, and photos of his drivers also appeared on the screen. He went back to the table and his hands were shaking.

"Aarif, we have a big problem," he whispered. "I just saw on the TV news the car descriptions and photos of our drivers. I don't know where they got that information."

"What! That's not possible. Did they mention a bombing at the Maine Mall?"

"Aarif, lower your voice." At that moment the waitress came with their food, and Ben said nothing until she left the table.

"I don't know where the cops got the information, but we need to eat up and get on our way to Canada," said Ben.

"This is horrible, Ben. All our months of planning and all the expense, and now the cops are looking for our drivers. What will we say to our foreign leaders? I gave my word that we could do this. My reputation is on the line. Oh, Ben, this can't be true."

"Aarif, some of this is beyond our control. Some of our people may get through to their targets. Even if they don't, they were instructed to take people with them if the cops stopped them. There yet could be some great explosions on the road."

"But Ben, why didn't the car blow up at the Mall? Is it possible it did, and the police have a news blackout?"

"No, the cops can't hide something like that, and the press would be all over the story. Something must have come apart, or maybe the timing isn't right and it will still blow up later today or tomorrow."

They paid for their food and left the restaurant. Before leaving the parking lot, Ben turned on the radio so they could listen to any bulletins about their operation. He also looked around to see if there were any police cars in the area. Seeing none, he started out to get on Route 2 west towards Vermont.

"Did you see if our vehicle was on the TV news?" asked Aarif.

"I didn't see it, but I didn't want to stop and watch the whole news report, in case someone got suspicious of me. I do think it best that we head for Canada today and not stop at Burlington for the night."

"Yes, we need to get out of the country and see what develops. I hope this doesn't lead the police to the mosque in New Jersey. I promised Sheikh Al Sakhr our plan was foolproof. He will be furious with us."

"Right now, Aarif, we need to save ourselves and get out of the country. "

୶

Lt. Goss did have his negotiator try to get the driver to answer him. They were using the loudspeaker, since Goss didn't want his officers getting close to the car. However, the driver refused to say anything. He just sat in the car.

"I have him on the scope," said the SWAT team leader. "He keeps looking at his watch. I wonder if he has a delayed explosive device on that bomb?"

୶

West of Gorham, New Hampshire Sheriff Manner had deployed three cars and a fire engine along an open, flat area of Route 2. If the terrorists tried to go around, they would end up in open fields on either side of the road. There were no buildings or people in the area. He chose this position in case there was a gunfight. Two of the sheriff's sharpshooters were positioned on the fire engine. He also sent two police vehicles off on a side road about a half-mile from the intended barricade. Their job was to become a blocking force if the terrorists tried to turn back to Gorham. He had Deputy Cobb switch to an unmarked police vehicle so that he could watch the Subjects at a distance and keep the officers apprised of their position. It didn't take long for Cobb to report that they were just about a mile from the barricade.

୶

At the barricade in York, Maine, the police negotiator repeatedly tried to get Nasir to speak with him. He finally gave up and suggested to Lt. Goss that they try to find an Arabic speaker to see if the Subject would respond to that person. While Goss was discussing this with Bowman at the Operations Center, Nasir got out of the car. He opened the rear door and reached in for his explosive vest. He put it on and pushed the plunger. Nothing happened!

"Put down that vest and put up your hands," said a voice from behind the barricade. Nasir just gave a sullen look while he threw the vest towards the barricade. "Hold you fire," said Goss.

Nasir slumped to the ground on his knees and started to speak in the Arabic language.

"I think he's praying," said the SWAT team leader.

"Send two men out and grab him while he is away from the car," said Goss. "If he pulls out a weapon, take him down."

∽

Back at the Operations Center in Portland, Hartley asked a question that was on the mind of several people. "If this guy is at the York tolls, where are the other three cars?"

"We don't see them on the Turnpike," said Bowman. "There are spotters on the overhead roads going north and south on the Turnpike, and they haven't reported any sightings."

"It's possible they are using secondary roads, but the only major one heading south is Route 1," said Daniels.

"But I'll bet it is crowded with holiday traffic," said Patrick.

"That is a problem," said Daniels. "Route 1 goes through all the towns south of Portland, and there usually is congestion getting through them. They may have slipped down through that corridor and picked up I-95 in New

Hampshire, thinking they would be safer than using the Turnpike."

"If they used Route 1, there are two bridges leading across into New Hampshire they could take, and we don't have any police spotters at those bridges," said Bowman.

"Let's tell the New Hampshire State Police that they may have come that way and to alert the police in the towns along Route 1," said Hartley. "Even with the congestion, they could be out of Maine by now, and our best chance of finding them may be in New Hampshire or Massachusetts."

"I'll take care of that," said Bowman.

⁊

Ben and Aarif were driving west on Route 2, and Ben made sure to stay within the speed limits. There was light traffic, but Ben kept a constant watch for police cars. They came down a hill and into a flatland area with open fields. Off in the distance, Ben could see a fire truck and cars with flashing lights. He thought perhaps there was an accident. However, to be cautious, he searched ahead to see if there were any side roads he could take but saw none. As he looked back in his mirror, he did see two police cars coming up behind him, and he wondered if they were heading towards the accident. However, they were not flashing their lights and didn't seem to be in a hurry. "We may have police company, Aarif. There are two police cars behind us, and that may or may not be an accident up ahead."

"What do we do, Ben? You think they are looking for us?"

"I don't know, but we need to be prepared. When we get closer, if it looks like a real accident, we will slow down and follow the police directions. If it's a trap, I want you to start

298

firing at the cops while I drive around them through the open field on the left."

"We can't out-run them, Ben."

"Well, if you have a better plan, spit it out now. Just keep firing when I tell you. These are county cops and may not know how to react to us attacking them. If we can evade them, I'll find a farm or store where we can steal a car to continue our trip."

As they approached what looked like an accident scene, Ben sensed this was a trap. He saw a police officer motioning for them to stop. Ben slowed the SUV as they neared the roadblock and then suddenly floored the car and headed for the field on the left side. "Start firing now, Aarif!" he shouted.

Aarif put the automatic weapon out the window and started firing blindly. He had no idea what he was doing or even the caliber of the weapon he was firing. He just knew how to pull the trigger. However, this was a fatal mistake. Police officers dove for cover. The two sharp shooters on the fire truck opened up, causing the Toyota to veer off the road and flip over. The firing stopped, and the police surrounded the vehicle. Bending down, one of the officers said, "I think our boys fired bull's eyes sheriff. These two look dead to me."

"We will let the coroner provide the official death notice," said Sheriff Manner. "In the meantime, haul these two out of the car and ID them. The Homeland Security guys will want that information. The State Police are sending over their crime scene unit, and I'll notify the boys in Portland that we have eliminated one of their problems."

᪉

Despite having left the farm in 15-minute intervals, Rabiah Abdou found himself behind Naseef Al Shuaibi as they drove slowly through the town of Kennebunk. The congestion on Route 1 was heavy, and Naseef had made more stops along the way than Rabiah. Both drivers had begun to relax as they proceeded down Route 1 and crossed over into New Hampshire. No one seemed to pay any attention to them, and the traffic was filled with out-of-state tourists. So they decided to travel together. They joined Interstate 95 south of the Hampton Tolls in New Hampshire and proceeded on to Massachusetts.

∽

At the York Tolls in Maine, Nasir Ahmed was taken into custody without a fight. He appeared to be praying when he was apprehended and refused to answer any questions. He was brought to Portland for booking and turned over to the US Marshalls. He also refused to talk with the DHS agents. Hartley and Patrick considered bringing in Ayman Siede to see if he could engage him.

∽

Sheriff Manner called the Operations Center and gave them the news of the deaths of Ben and Aarif. Hartley dispatched DHS agents to New Hampshire to see what information could be gleaned from a search of the SUV they were driving. While all this was taking place, Captain Bowman reported that the bomb squad had examined both the vest and the bomb in the car at the York Toll Plaza. Again, it was discovered that the explosives were put together correctly, but that there were no detonating charges."

Someone obviously removed or never inserted detonators into the explosive devices," said Patrick. "Do you think there was a mole in their operation?"

"From what the woman at the farm told our agents, it must have been the bomb maker," said Hartley. "This guy Ghanem saved the woman and didn't blow up the house, so he must have had a falling-out with the leaders. When they searched the barn, they did find detonators. At first they thought these were extras, but now it may be that this Ghanem rigged the bombs and didn't put in detonators."

"If all these other guys knew nothing about explosives, he could have pulled this off," said John Carver.

"Well, let's hope this is the case," said Patrick. "However, we still have three cars out there, and we don't have any reporting."

∽

Umar and his brother Awad Hussein had successfully driven down Route 1 and into New Hampshire. However, they had been listening to the radio and were shocked when a news alert gave descriptions of the cars and their names. Despite having volunteered to help Aarif, they had no intention of being arrested by American authorities. Using his smart phone, Umar got directions to Logan Airport in Boston. They decided to put the car in a parking area at the airport and set the timer for the explosion to occur in twelve hours. Their plan was to take the shuttle to New York and a bus to Kennedy International Airport. They knew a private charter aircraft could be rented to take them to the UK. They could pay for the charter with their father's business account, and their names would not be checked against any Homeland Security lists.

❧

Naseef and Rabiah had no trouble driving into Massachusetts and south along the Route 128 corridor of Interstate 95. With hand signals, they decided to stop at the next service area for food and fuel. What they did not know was they had been spotted by an officer in an unmarked Massachusetts State Police vehicle, and that other officers were being directed to the chase. When they reached a service area, they exited and parked the cars, preferring to eat before refueling. This was opportune for the police, since they were able to set up an apprehension plan for when the two exited the restaurant and before they reached their cars.

❧

The report of spotting the two cars by the Massachusetts State Police was welcome news in the Operations Center. Captain Bowman had two of his officers doing time and distance scenarios, trying to get a geographical grid as to where the last vehicle could be located. Since the Hussein brothers had been students in this country, the theory was they were probably more adept at using our road system. Based on the sighting of the two cars in Massachusetts, the officers thought the last car could be down into Connecticut or heading west to New York State. Another BOLO was sent out to all police agencies in New England, giving an update on the captures, and asking everyone to focus on the car driven by the Hussein brothers. There could be no let-up until this last car was found.

❧

Destiny Carter had been sent to stay overnight with her friend Ginny Paine, while the police and DHS agents searched the Carter farm and property with the help of John Hartwell, who maintained the farm when Destiny was not in residence. At Patrick's suggestion, Scott Hartley arranged to have Nola Hunter flown up to Portland the next day and assist with the continuing interview of Destiny. They planned to do the interview in Portland, while the police and agents finished the search of her farm. So far, all that had been uncovered were fingerprints of people who had been there.

CHAPTER FIFTY

The Hussein brothers arrived at Logan Airport and elected to leave the car in the economy parking area, and then take the airport bus to the US Airways terminal to catch the shuttle to New York. The timer was set for the car to explode in twelve hours, and they believed the explosion would cause panic and disrupt flight operations. It was getting late into the afternoon by the time they reached the terminal and paid for their plane tickets. They choose the shuttle to New York because numerous people flew the shuttle without an advanced reservation, and passengers seldom had checked baggage. The ticket purchase went smoothly, and they proceeded through security without any problem.

Later that afternoon, Jeff Propes finished his shift as an airport bus driver and headed for a pre-arranged social with some college friends at The Landing, a bar on Long Wharf on the Boston waterfront. Jeff was a college student at Boston College, and driving a bus around the terminals and parking areas at Logan was his summer job. Jeff arrived late because of the congestion at the Ted Williams tunnel, and his friends were on their second round when he arrived. Since there was no radio in his airport bus, he had missed the day's news events. Everyone was talking about the chase to catch the terrorists driving cars with bombs and the fact that one car and two of the terrorists were still on the run. As the hourly news came on the TV, the crowd quieted some, and Jeff joined his friends to hear the latest news. When they flashed the photos of the Hussein brothers on the screen, Jeff almost dropped his beer. "I saw those guys!" he shouted. "They were on my bus."

"Don't give Jeff another drink," one of his friends shouted.

"Screw you," he said. "Those guys were on my bus late this afternoon. I dropped them at the US Airways shuttle."

"Hey, they look just like a lot of other Arabs with beards," another friend said. "You probably see hundreds of guys that look like that every day at the airport."

"No, I'm sure it is them."

"How can you be so sure?" asked the friend.

"They were the only two on my bus from the economy parking to the terminal. I tried to talk with them, but they just acted nervous and ignored me. They didn't have any luggage and were sitting up front. I got a good look at them. That's them!"

"Well, if you're so sure, let's call the police," one of his female friends said. She dialed up 911 and said to the operator, "I have a friend here who says he saw the two terrorists the police are searching for. What should we do?"

"Where are we? What is all that noise? We are in a bar."

"No, we are quite sober, operator. We just stopped to have a few drinks before dinner, and our friend who drives a bus at Logan said he saw the two guys they just showed on the TV."

"How does he know it's them? Well, he says the two guys on the TV screen were on his bus, and he recognized them. You want to talk to him?"

Jeff took the phone and told the 911 operator what he had told his friends. After assurances they were sober, the operator took his name and the bar where they were drinking and told him a patrol would be there in a few minutes.

An hour later, Jeff was showing the police and DHS agents the area of the parking lot where he had picked up the two males that afternoon. A search of the parking area ensued, and, in short order, they found the missing vehicle. The bomb squad was dispatched, while Jeff accompanied the officers to the terminal where he had dropped the suspects.

∽

There was jubilation in the Operations Center when Hartley announced the news of the discovery of the last vehicle. This vehicle, like the others, had been rigged for explosives, but no detonating charges were found.

US Airways confirmed that two males by the names of Umar and Awad Hussein had boarded the 4:00 PM shuttle for LaGuardia airport in New York City. Since no BOLO information had been reported to the airlines, the Hussein brothers had been processed like any other shuttle passenger. Hartley later stated that DHS should have notified the airlines, even though they were looking for vehicles.

While all the vehicles were accounted for and the explosives were contained, they still needed to find the Hussein brothers. The search was now directed at the New York City area. Alerts were sent out to airports in the New York area, and DHS agents were sent to LaGuardia.

"I'll bet they are trying to fly out on an international flight," said Patrick.

"I agree," said Hartley. "We missed them at LaGuardia. The shuttle arrived before we knew they were on the plane.

We are now showing their photos to everyone at LaGuardia, but haven't had any hits yet."

"If I recall correctly, you can take a bus from LaGuardia to Kennedy," said John Carver.

"You're correct," said Hartley. 'We are questioning bus drivers, but you know how it is in the late afternoon rush hours. We also are canvassing the international terminals at Kennedy, but no luck so far."

"They might try to book a charter," said Patrick. "Their father is very wealthy, and it would be safer for them, since they don't have to go through all the security we have for the regular airlines."

"I agree and have told our supervisor at Kennedy to send someone over to the private charter terminal. We need to get more photos around too. We will get them! " Hartley proceed to go around the room and thank all the state, local, and federal officers for their great cooperation and support. He capped it off by stating that he was buying at the Old Port tonight.

EPILOGUE

Nola Hunter assisted in the debriefing of Destiny Carter for two days. Both she and the other agents believed Destiny was more involved than she admitted, but she had her story together and never diverted from it. With the deaths of Ben and Aarif, there was no one to refute her version of the events. She later went back to California to finish law school.

∽

Ghanem disappeared into the Caribbean islands and, despite numerous tips and leads, had not been heard from over the past few years. When his photo was circulated amongst federal agencies, the local FBI office in Detroit responded that one Leroy Smith had been a confidential informant for the Bureau, reporting on radical Islamists in the Detroit area. He had learned to be a cook in prison and was employed as such when released from prison. He worked with the local FBI office for almost eight months but suddenly dropped from sight. Inquiries amongst his friends and family proved negative. Apparently, he had volunteered to work for the Bureau in exchange for a reduced sentence from prison.

∽

Samir Dahar was lucky. The victim in the bar fight never showed up in court, and the charges were dropped. Samir was debriefed for several weeks in a DHS safe house. He agreed to be a confidential source for DHS and was sent back to the bakery and his lady friend in St. Maarten.

∽

The Hussein brothers were not so lucky. When DHS checked their names at the private aircraft terminal at

Kennedy, the names were not on any manifests. However, when viewing the photos at the Transatlantic Charter Company, the manager said the two were passengers using different names and were currently on a flight to Heathrow. The plane had been chartered and paid for by the Bright Desert Star Holding Company, which was owned by their father. The brothers were surprised when landing at Heathrow. Instead of the normal Immigration and Customs officials, they were met by officers from the Metropolitan police and held for pending deportation back to the United States.

∽

The Husseins and the other drivers were subsequently tried in Federal Court in Boston and are serving long sentences for their part in this terrorist operation. None of them ever talked or admitted their guilt, contending they were "set up" and targeted because of their Muslim faith.

∽

Professor Akil Hakimi did return to Egypt for a few weeks and did bring his family back to Burlington. He never came under suspicion for compromising Aarif's operation and continues to be a covert source for DHS. Due to the turmoil in Egypt, Hakimi has extended his time in the States as an exchange professor.

∽

At DHS, Richard Sandelman decided to retire, and Melissa Wallis was promoted to Chief of the Current Analysis Branch. The Berwick Group continues to work with DHS, but Nola finds that Patrick is spending more time in Maine, enjoying the outdoor activities the state has to offer. She doesn't mind, since she and her children often get to visit there, too.

CPSIA information can be obtained at www.ICGtesting.com
Printed in the USA
BVOW07s0058271014

372444BV00001B/22/P